More Short Prayers for public worship

Nick Fawcett

kevin mayhew

kevin mayhew

First published in Great Britain in 2012 by Kevin Mayhew Ltd
Buxhall, Stowmarket, Suffolk IP14 3BW
Tel: +44 (0) 1449 737978 Fax: +44 (0) 1449 737834
E-mail: info@kevinmayhewltd.com

www.kevinmayhew.com

ISBN 978 1 84867 499 8
Catalogue No. 1501335

Cover design by Rob Mortonson

Typeset by Richard Weaver

Printed and bound in Great Britain

Contents

Foreword

'Let us pray.' In some quarters those words are greeted with a subconscious sigh. Why? Because the ensuing prayer can at times rival the sermon in length – and, in nonconformist churches at least, that's no mean feat! Longer still were some of the extemporary prayers I used to hear as a boy, several of them guaranteed to last for anything up to quarter of an hour, ranging over just about any and every subject you could imagine. Those who offered such prayers were lovely people, don't get me wrong – deeply committed and unquestionably sincere – but somehow they just couldn't stop their tongues from running away with them.

Lengthy prayers no doubt have their place – I myself have written and prayed a few in my time! – but prayer is an activity in which brevity can be a definite virtue. We have that on the highest authority, Jesus himself urging people 'not to pile up pointless phrases as the Gentiles do, imagining God will listen to them because of their many words' (Matthew 6:7). Paradoxically, those who communicate most effectively are often those who say the least, and vice versa.

Many of us probably already apply the words of Jesus in our devotional lives, albeit inadvertently, offering up brief single-sentence prayers to articulate the mood of a moment rather than attempting anything more eloquent. Partly this is down to constraints on time, but it's also because it feels natural. Prayer, after all, is meant to be a conversation, not a monologue, and if God is going to speak he needs the opportunity to get a word in.

In the context of public worship, other factors come into play. With the best will in the world, many will find their attention starting to wander if prayers go on for too long. I speak from experience, having come perilously close on a few occasions to nodding off during particularly loquacious intercessions. With such considerations in mind, during my time in the ministry I took to using two or three short prayers of intercession, much as Anglicans and Catholics use brief collects rather than a single 'long prayer'. Instead of attempting to cover every issue in the world, I focused on a few needs and situations, tying these in as far as possible with the theme of the service.

The prayers in this book – drawn and adapted from my books *The Animal Lover's Prayer Book; Touching the Seasons; Heaven Touching Earth;*

Touching Down; Touched by His Hand; For You and for Many; Calling Venus; Calling Mars and *Celebrating Grandparents* – are not intended to serve as the principal prayers in a service of public worship. They are designed, rather, to sum up and commit to God a particular area of life or faith, and as such they can be used in different ways and at different points in the service. Some lend themselves to the close of worship and others to its opening. Some will fit well at the end of a sermon, others in consecrating an offering, others again as prayers of approach, and others still as short intercessions or expressions of praise and confession. You may find yet other ways of using them. Arranged in alphabetical sections, they cover a wide range of themes, spanning daily life and relationships, the journey of discipleship, grace before meals, Christian seasons, hope and trust, joy and celebration, a host of intercessions, and much more. All, though, have one thing in common. They are offered as a way of simply, concisely, yet sincerely committing our lives and worship to God in prayer. I hope and pray that they may help do just that.

Nick Fawcett

The Bible

1 Almighty God, teach us not just to *read* the Scriptures, but to *study* them, seeking your way, your will, your word. Amen.

2 Thank you, Lord God, for the Bible; for its testimony to your dealings with your people and the unfolding of your purpose across the ages. Help us to read it and to understand. Amen.

3 Merciful God, you have given us your word, the good news of Christ. Teach us not just to *read* the Scriptures, but to *study* them, searching there for your way, your will. Give us diligence to persist, wisdom to understand, openness to receive and courage to respond. Amen.

Blessings

4 God go with us and with all whom we love – a constant source of help, hope and happiness, today and always. Amen.

5 The God who blesses us so richly, leads us so surely, forgives us so freely, supports us so staunchly and loves us so completely, go with us, now and always. Amen.

6 May the Christ who died for us, live in us; the Christ who loves us, shine through us; the Christ who welcomes us, go with us, this and every day. Amen.

7 May the love of Christ shine in our eyes, the compassion of Christ work through our hands, the word of Christ fall from our lips and the life of Christ flow through our veins, to his glory. Amen.

8 Lord Jesus Christ, as you have served, so may we serve in turn; as you have loved, so may we love in turn; as you have cared, so may we care in turn; as you have lived, so may we live in turn; until that day when we are one with you and your people everywhere, and you are all in all. Amen.

9 May God guide you in all you think, say and do, so that you may know his will and walk in his way, this day and always. Amen.

10 Living God, be in our loving and living, our speaking and serving, our working and resting, our dying and rising. Be all in all in us, through Jesus Christ our Lord. Amen.

11 May the giver of life sustain us as we offer him our service. May the giver of life go with us as we celebrate all he has given. May the source of life guide us as we walk in his way. And may the resurrection and the life, Jesus Christ our Lord, bless and keep us, now and for all eternity. Amen.

12 Day by day, O God, may the living Christ speak *to* us, grow *in* us, work *through* us, shine *from* us and dwell *with* us. Amen.

13 Living God, may love continue to fill us and grace continue to thrill us as we return to the daily business of life. May we give without reserve, and live resolved to serve, so that the ordinary may be touched by the divine, each moment consecrated to you and sanctified by your touch. Amen.

14 Give thanks for the past, celebrate the present, trust in God's future, and may his unfailing love surround you, your loved ones and all the world, now and for evermore. Amen.

15 Lord Jesus of Bethlehem, be born in us. Lord Jesus of Galilee, speak to us. Lord Jesus of Gethsemane, strengthen us in times of trial. Lord Jesus of Calvary, support us, even in suffering and death. Lord Jesus of the empty tomb, grant us life in all its fullness. Lord of heaven and earth, may our lives bring honour to your name, now and always. Amen.

16 May God bless and keep us, together with all our loved ones, everywhere we go and in everything we do. Amen.

17 Let us go in God's name, showing how much he means to us through the way we live and the people we are. Amen.

Call of God

see also Voice of God

18 Almighty God, you called, but somehow we cut you off. Forgive us, and help us to get back in touch. Amen.

19 Gracious God, whatever you ask us to do, wherever you ask us to go, help us to respond to your call, and follow where you lead. Amen.

20 Almighty God, we can't explain your call, for there's so much about it we don't understand, so much about you, about faith, about life itself, that leaves us searching for answers; troubled, confused, uncertain. And yet your summons rings true, your invitation to know and love you finding an echo in our hearts, answering some primal need deep within, and until we respond we can find no rest. Help us, fully and faithfully, to commit ourselves to you, and to follow where you lead. Amen.

21 Rouse us to your call, Lord – your summons to faith, service, repentance and commitment, however disturbing it may be. Instead of sleepwalking through life, ignoring what we'd rather not face, may we hear your voice and wake up to your challenge, ready to live each day for you. Amen.

22 Lord of all, increase our love and strengthen our commitment, so that wherever you ask us to go and whatever you want us to do, we will respond gladly and faithfully fulfil your will. Amen.

23 Lord Jesus Christ, help us to bear your name with pride, our lives, like the cross, shining as a sign of your love and emblem of your grace. Help us to live up to your call and never to disgrace it; to play our part faithfully in the work of your kingdom, so as to bring honour and glory to you. Amen.

Challenges, facing

24 Loving God, forgive us, for too often we run away from a challenge for fear of making a fool of ourselves. Remind us that it's better to attempt something and fall flat on our face than never to attempt it at all. Amen.

25 Almighty God, help us, for we walk a fine line between faith and doubt, belief and unbelief, our commitment being less secure than we like to pretend. Give us a sure and certain faith, able to meet whatever challenges life might bring and still to stand firm. Amen.

26 Gracious God, when we're uncertain of the way ahead, the journey of life presenting unexpected difficulties and dangers, give us courage to walk in faith, trusting you to lead us. However unsteady our progress and daunting the challenge before us, teach us to take one step at a time and to leave the rest to you. Amen.

27 Lord of all, remind us that you are a God of surprises, constantly overturning the expectations of this world, turning weakness to strength, despair to hope and defeat to victory. Teach us, then, however much we feel up against it, however daunting the challenge and feeble our resources, to trust in you, knowing that nothing finally will be able to frustrate your will or deny the triumph of your love. Amen.

28 Almighty God, teach us to persevere, not being discouraged by the obstacles we meet along the way but recognising them as integral to the course set before us, each a new challenge to be faced with you. However stiff the test or depleted our reserves, help us to battle on and run our race to the very end. Amen.

29 Lord Jesus Christ, thank you that whatever challenge we face, you have gone ahead to prepare the way; that whatever the future may hold, you will be there to meet and greet us. Amen.

30 Sovereign God, we thought we could cope with whatever challenges life might bring, but we realise now that we're not as strong as we thought. What we cannot carry alone help us to shoulder with you. Amen.

31 Almighty God, whatever obstacles life brings, whatever challenges and hurdles, give us strength to meet them, the assurance that what we *can't* do, you *can*! Amen.

32 When life brings us down with a bump, Lord, save us from feeling sorry for ourselves. Help us to get up and try again, until we finally succeed. Amen.

Christian seasons

Advent

33 Living God, help us in all our preparations for Christmas – the writing of cards, buying of presents, wrapping of gifts, decorating of the home – to make ready for you, preparing ourselves in heart and mind to worship you afresh and welcome you more fully into our lives, so that when the day of your coming finally dawns, we may be ready to greet you and truly celebrate, not on *our* terms but on *yours*. Amen.

34 Gracious God, it's hard sometimes to keep faith that your kingdom will come, for so much in the world seems to deny your love and frustrate your will. However hard it may be, though, help us to trust in your promises, daring to believe the day will come, despite everything that conspires against it, when your love finally triumphs over all. Amen.

35 Almighty God, you tell us to look forward, anticipating the dawn of your kingdom. We've no idea when that will be or what it will mean, but, however long the wait, teach us to look forward expectantly, assured that the day *will* come: a day that will transform not only our lives, but the whole world, for ever. Amen.

36 Eternal God, remind us that you alone truly know the future, your promises of old having found fulfilment in Christ, the message of the Law and prophets being vindicated by his birth, death and resurrection. Help us, remembering all you have so faithfully done, to trust in all you will yet do, confident that, in the fullness of time, your purpose will be accomplished and your kingdom will dawn. Amen.

37 Awesome God, save us from carelessness in our relationship with you, from being casual and complacent in our dealings, assuming we can gloss over whatever's wrong between us. Teach us to work at our faith, preparing the ground each day to know you better, so that when your kingdom comes we may be ready to stand before you and meet you, face to face. Amen.

38 Gracious God, teach us that your coming into the world was not without cost; that you gave of yourself, surrendering your life to bring us light. Help us, as we celebrate your birth, to remember also your death and to be ready in turn to give as well as receive in the service of your kingdom. Amen.

39 Lord Jesus Christ, though we speak of your coming again, your return to establish your kingdom, it's hard to anticipate it meaningfully, and part of us doesn't want to, for you've given so much here and now that's good, and it would seem wrong to overlook this life through dwelling on the next. Yet don't let us lose altogether our sense of expectation; the conviction that one day your will shall be done – sorrow overcome, evils righted, love triumphant, death itself destroyed. Help us to celebrate today in the light of your tomorrow. Amen.

40 Lord Jesus, we like to think we're ready for your return – to serve you, respond to your call and welcome you when you come again – but are we actually anywhere near it, or has the life that coursed within us drained away, energy and enthusiasm dissipated, leaving behind a discipleship that flatters to deceive? Come, and fill us afresh, so that we may live and work for you. Amen.

41 Almighty God, forgive us, for so often we're disobedient, ignoring your call and defying your will, preferring our way to yours. Teach us, instead, like Mary long ago, to listen to your voice and, humbly, to obey, putting your will before our own – self second and you first. Amen.

Christmas

42 Gracious God, at this time of giving and receiving, help us to share the message of your love – a gift not just for us but for all. Whatever things we keep to ourselves, may the good news of your coming not be among them. Amen.

43 Almighty God, help us at this season, to go in heart and mind to Bethlehem – to the stable, the manger, the baby in the straw – so that your Son, our saviour, may be born again, in us. Amen.

44 Living God, despite the glitz, bustle, hype and expense, Christmas proves a let-down for many, promising much yet delivering little. Awaken the hearts of all to the glorious surprise at its heart – the wonder of your Son, born in a stable and laid in a manger, your Word made flesh and love incarnate – a gift beyond price that will never disappoint. Amen.

45 Redeemer God, for so many people Christmas stirs a sense of your presence, reminding them of a reality beyond this world, a relationship they crave, and for a few days churches bulge at the seams as carols are sung and the gospel message is given a hearing . . . but then January sales beckon, calling folk back to their true devotion, and you are forgotten again for another year. Break through the trappings of this season and touch human hearts the world over, so that instead of being just briefly remembered, you may be known and loved, this and every day. Amen.

46 Living God, save us from frittering away our money at Christmas on trivia, while a world goes hungry; from turning this season of goodwill to *all* into one of good things for *us*. Teach us to make room in our celebrations for those who, in this life, have so little to celebrate and to give as generously to them as we have so richly received. Amen.

47 Merciful God, forgive us, for we mistake the material trappings of this season for the real thing, confusing show with substance, ornament with essence. Help us to see beyond the glitz to the true meaning of Christmas. Amen.

48 Loving God, help us to remember that whatever we receive this Christmas, it can never compare with that greatest gift of all: your coming among us in Christ. Amen.

49 Lord God, help us to see beyond the trappings and traditions of this season to the awesome truth they proclaim: your Word, your Son, your love, your gift, good news, now and always. Amen.

50 Gracious God, how much time will we make for you this Christmas? How much time, before, during and after the celebrations, to reflect on your love? Will we be able to measure it in hours, days, or will it be just brief snatches, a moment here and there included almost as an afterthought? Forgive us, for all too often, at Christmas or otherwise, we have time for just about everything . . . except you. Amen.

51 Almighty God, in the rush and bustle of this season, with so much to remember and such a lot to do, teach us to make time simply to pause and to ponder what it all means. Amen.

52 Living God, keep alive the magic of this season, an awareness of the mystery at its heart. Though we lose our childish illusions, may we retain a youthful sense of wonder at your coming among us in Christ. Amen.

53 Sovereign God, open our hearts to the radiance of your love, the light that shone in the birth of your Son and that continues to shine today, nothing able to overcome it. Help us to glimpse afresh the true romance of this season, the full wonder and beauty of it all, able to shed light in our hearts not just at Christmas but each moment of every day. Amen.

54 Loving God, remind us that after the stable came a cross, after birth, death, after celebration, sacrifice, and after pleasure, pain, each expressing a single theme: the wonder of your love. Help us to rejoice in all that this season means, not just in part but in full. Amen.

55 Teach us, Lord God, amid the festivity and merriment of this season, to delve deeper, discovering what's of real value within it: the new life you offer through your Son, bringing nourishment to body, mind and soul. Help us to receive for ourselves that most precious gift of all. Amen.

56 Almighty God, teach us to put you at the centre of Christmas, so that you can transform our lives – the things we do, the way we think, the people we are, each touched by your presence and made new by your love. Amen.

57 Gracious God, thank you for the closeness you have made possible through your Son, not just with others but above all with you. Thank you for the relationship we can enjoy with you through your coming among us in Christ, sharing our humanity and dying our death to bring us life. Help us to celebrate the love at the heart of this season and, through him, draw us closer to you each day. Amen.

58 Lord of all, thank you for the message of Christmas, so familiar and well loved yet still able to surprise us with joy, causing us to catch our breath in wonder. Amen.

59 Almighty God, though much of the packaging surrounding Christmas needs discarding, having nothing to do with its true meaning, save us from overlooking the love and care you showed in preparing the way of Christ. Help us, if we would fully celebrate your gift, to appreciate the context in which you gave it – the history of your people, the teaching of the Law and the message of the prophets, each finding glorious fulfilment in the Word made flesh. For your Son, and all that points to your love shown through him, thank you! Amen.

60 Through this Christmas season, Lord, as we wrap and unwrap our presents, teach us what it means to give and receive – to open our hearts not just to loved ones, but to others and to you. Amen.

61 Living God, we grow tired of most things eventually, even those that are special; what we greeted once with joy and gratitude we can end up viewing with disdain. Forgive our over-familiarity with the wonder of your love and help us still to celebrate the good news of Christ – something to go on getting excited about, day after day. Amen.

62 Whatever else we grow out of, Lord, help us to keep faith in you, who alone gives meaning not just to Christmas, but to all. Amen.

Epiphany

63 Great and glorious God, forgive us, for we repeatedly obscure your light, stopping it from both shining in or out. Pull back the curtains we close against you, so that the light of your love and radiance of your presence may flood into our hearts and out through our lives. Amen.

64 Almighty God, in the darkest moments of life, the darkest places, the darkest experiences, bring your love, your life, your light. Amen.

65 Gracious God, thank you for the new day you bring through the rising of your Son, the new beginnings, new life, you daily make possible through him. Thank you for your promise that, however deep the darkness may seem, light will dawn again, shining in our hearts for evermore. Amen.

66 Living God, you have brought light to our lives, illuminating each day with your love. Shine in and through us, so that we may help to bring a little light in turn to others. Amen.

67 Thank you, Lord God, for your light, guiding to Bethlehem, shining from Christ, pouring from the empty tomb and sparkling in our hearts. Thank you for the knowledge that, whatever life brings, you will give light to our path, this and every day. Amen.

Lent *see also* Stillness and quiet

68 Lord God, how often do we give thought to what comprises our life, carefully weighing the ingredients in the balance to ensure we've got them right? Too often we become casual, complacent, settling for whatever's on offer, without a second thought. Whatever else we overlook this season, teach us to make room for the things that really matter; room, above all, for you. Amen.

69 Almighty God, examine us and help us to see where our faith is weak and our lives are lacking. Put a new heart and a right spirit within us, and make us whole. Amen.

70 Living God, we don't want to neglect our body, for it is your gift, but what of our soul, the inner self? Teach us to seek wholeness of spirit with equal resolve, to work for true well-being, cultivating a health that will neither fade nor perish. Amen.

71 Holy and righteous God, test us and know our hearts. Examine us and search our thoughts. Delve deep within and cleanse us from all that fragments our faith and undermines our commitment, preventing us from living as you intend. Redeem, renew, restore. Amen.

72 Generous God, help us to give something up for Lent, not because it's expected or out of empty show but to promote our spiritual health. Enable us, with your help, to cut out whatever undermines our discipleship, denying your love and frustrating your purpose; whatever, in other words, creates a barrier between us, preventing us from knowing you as we should and could. Amen.

73 Almighty God, help us to see where our relationship with you is not as it should be, not as secure or as close as we like to think. However trivial our faults may seem, save us from taking them too lightly – from putting off tackling them for so long that we slip up once too often and fall completely from your side. Amen.

74 Loving God, examine us and make us whole. Put a new heart and right spirit within us, and restore us in body, mind and spirit. Come now and transform our lives by your healing, redeeming touch. Amen.

75 Lord, we find the promise of immediate pleasure, instant gratification, hard to resist, but you offer eternal sustenance, nourishing deep within. Teach us to long for what truly satisfies – to hunger, above all, for you. Amen.

76 Sovereign God, test us and know our thoughts. Search us, and help us to see where we're spiritually weak, our faith lacking and our commitment poor. Put a new heart and a right spirit within us, and, by your grace, make us whole. Amen.

77 Gracious God, keep us alert to whatever threatens our faith, to perils – seen and unseen – that endanger the life we've found in you. Remind us that though you will do your bit, equally we must do ours. Amen.

78 Like a moth, Lord, we are attracted by what destroys, promising life yet delivering death. We try to fight it, aware of the danger, but the lure is too strong, all sense forgotten when temptation strikes. Draw us close to you, and shine in our darkness, bringing the light that leads to life. Amen.

79 Almighty God, though we can control some things, others, if we give them the chance, will finally control us. Teach us to see things for what they are, and to act accordingly. Amen.

80 Merciful God, examine us and show us what's wrong in our lives. Search us and help us to recognise where we go astray. Teach us to look carefully at who and what we are, identifying our faults and weaknesses, and, with your help, seeking to put them right, so that, imperfect as we are, we may nonetheless draw a little closer to what we're meant to be and what we hunger to become. Amen.

81 Lord Jesus Christ, we talk too glibly of sacrifice and self-denial, when in reality we live almost wholly for our own ends, unwilling to surrender even a little for you or others, and through our failure to deny ourselves we daily deny you. Give us a genuine commitment to Christ that shows itself in action; a faith that makes a difference to who and what we are, unmistakable to all. Amen.

82 Almighty God, may your love keep hold of us in the daily round of life. Though we're buffeted by temptation and exposed to the wind of change, save us from being tossed about by the restless current. Secure us through your love so that we shall not go astray. Amen.

83 Lord Jesus Christ, teach us not to be taken in by what looks appealing but finally destroys, what promises satisfaction yet ultimately poisons within. However enticing temptation may be, help us to see where it might lead and to avoid its hidden dangers. Amen.

84 Almighty God, save us from courting disaster – from praying 'deliver us from evil', only to put ourselves in harm's way. Remind us that for *you* to play *your* part, we must play ours. Amen.

85 Teach us, Lord, that though some pleasures are innocent enough, what we might call 'naughty but nice', others are different. Help us to understand that the dangers they represent are greater than we realise and that any gratification they offer is less fulfilling than might first appear, either bringing happiness that doesn't last or being won at a cost to others, causing them hurt and sorrow. When temptation strikes, then, enable us to look beneath the surface, and beyond ourselves, and to consider where yielding might lead. Amen.

86 Gracious God, thank you for the relationship you have made possible – a relationship based not on fear but on love. Thank you that, mighty though you are, you care about our welfare and value us as friends. Amen.

87 Almighty God, too easily, and at this season in particular, we picture you with a frown on your face – stern, forbidding, angry – as though you are permanently displeased at our behaviour, looking for the opportunity to step in and condemn. Remind us that the reality is so very different, your nature being always to have mercy, to forgive, love and accept. Help us, then, during Lent and always, to celebrate your love that smiles upon us. Amen.

88 Merciful God, teach us that we can't have everything we want, that what we desire is not necessarily what we need. In moments of temptation, help us to know the difference. Amen.

89 Living God, too often the flame of our faith dies down, the commitment that once burned so brightly now barely smouldering, lofty intentions turned to ashes and ardour all but cold. Yet from the dying embers you bring new life, rekindling the fire of faith. Come now and reignite our love, so that it may burn afresh for you. Amen.

90 Loving God, we don't mean to mess things up; it just seems to happen, one thing leading to another. Teach us, before we act, to think first of the consequences. Amen.

91 Lord Jesus Christ, we remember how you had to choose in the wilderness between yourself and others – and how you chose the latter, knowing it would mean suffering and sacrifice, the agony of death on a cross, and knowing too that once you started out there could be no turning back. Help us to follow you with similar commitment, ready to walk your way to our journey's end. Amen.

92 Merciful God, when we go astray, feebly yielding to temptation, instead of laying the blame elsewhere, help us to see the devil in ourselves and, with your help, to change. Amen.

93 Lord God, teach us to weigh up our lives, assessing what goes into them and what comes out; to make time for work and rest, reflection and action, ourselves and others, this world and your kingdom. Teach us to find a place for all, keeping each in balance with the rest, so that, from the ingredients you've given, we may make the most of life, now and for all eternity. Amen.

94 Merciful God, it's not enough for us to say sorry when we go astray, for we've done that so often before, only to fail you again. Help us to show that we're serious, through actions as well as words. Amen.

95 Whenever we're tempted, Lord, and however attractive things may seem, help us to think carefully and to make the right decisions. Amen

96 Gracious God, teach us to use this season to set new targets, more ambitious goals, resolving to know, love and serve you better. Though we've failed before and will fail again, instead of being content merely to plod along may we truly strive to grow in grace. Amen.

Palm Sunday

97 Sovereign God, save us from worshipping ourselves, from glorying in our own wisdom, achievements or ends. In all we think, say and do, teach us to honour and serve you, the King of kings and Lord of lords. Amen.

98 Lord Jesus Christ, you know all about fickle allegiance, having heard your people's shouts of 'Hallelujah!' turn to cries of 'Crucify!' Our loyalty, too, is often found wanting when the chips are down. Though we profess undying commitment, we're like those who welcomed you into Jerusalem so long ago, swift to look the other way when commitment proves costly: denying or abandoning you when service involves sacrifice. Forgive the fragility of our faith, and give us an allegiance to you that stays true through thick and thin, just as you stay true to us. Amen.

99 When we're too full of ourselves, Lord, puffed up with our own importance, remind us that you revealed your glory not through a crown, but through a cross. Amen.

Holy Week

100 Living God, though we will always fall short, may something of Christ live within us: the faith with which he faced doubt in Gethsemane, the humility with which he met mockery from Herod, the courage with which he endured agony on the cross, the love with which he tackled hatred from his enemies, and the mercy with which he responded to those who took his life. May a little of these gifts be found in us, so that we may honour you more completely and work more effectively for your kingdom. Amen.

101 Thank you, Lord, for we were hungry, and you filled us. We have tasted your love and it's good beyond words. Amen.

102 Lord Jesus Christ, we were parched and you gave us something to drink: the water of life, quenching our thirst deep within. For that most special of gifts, thank you. Amen.

103 Lord Jesus, we remember today how Judas betrayed you, selling his very soul for thirty pieces of silver. Our price may be higher, but we're not as different as we like to think, money shaping our lives in all kinds of ways, controlling our thoughts and influencing our decisions, holding us under its spell. Forgive our foolish ways, for too often, without knowing it, we sell out to the highest bidder and betray you in turn. Amen.

104 Loving God, remind us that the cross of Christ speaks not merely of a single day but of *every* day, changing every moment and every*thing*. Help us more fully to understand and celebrate your grace, so that it may shape our lives, now and *always*. Amen.

105 Lord Jesus Christ, we recall today how you took a cup and proposed a 'toast': 'My blood, poured out for you and for many, for the forgiveness of sins.' A cup not of pleasure but of pain, drunk not for yourself but for others, representing the greatest of gifts, precious beyond words. Whenever we drink, remind us of the true vine and the new wine you offer to all. Amen.

106 Gracious God, speak afresh, to us and your world, of Christ and all he continues to mean; of the One who carried his cross in a different way, staggering under its weight until finally *it* carried *him*, writhing in agony as the life ebbed away. However familiar the cross may be, save us from taking it for granted and forgetting the awesome love of which it speaks. Amen.

107 Thank you, Lord, for pouring yourself out, turning the water of life into wine. Thank you that we can taste, and be satisfied, drink, and never thirst again. Help us, each day, to celebrate your love, your grace, your goodness, and to appreciate more fully the wonder of your gift, to us and to all. Amen.

108 Lord Jesus Christ, we remember today how nails were thrust deep into your hands and feet, inflicting not just surface wounds but ripping through flesh and crushing bone, the pain too dreadful to contemplate, never mind the agony soon to follow. For the immense love that could endure all this – willingly, gladly – for people such as us, receive our heartfelt praise. Amen.

109 Gracious God, thank you that though it was costly to make us yours, you paid the price and carried us safely home. Amen.

110 Redeemer God, we forget, too easily, that your Son was broken; that what he went through was no play-acting or sleight of hand, but suffering as real and terrible as we can imagine, endured until life was blotted out, seemingly ended for good. Teach us to remember that truth, but to remember also that such brokenness was not the end, for from death came life, from despair, hope and from sorrow, joy – your love bringing new beginnings. And remind us, above all, that this same love is *still* at work, able to take broken people, broken lives, and make them whole. Amen.

111 Eternal God, thank you that you are always with us, close by our side; that we can face the darkest moments of life, and even the shadow of death itself, with quiet confidence, knowing that you have been there before us and will see us safely through. Amen.

112 Lord Jesus Christ, you could have stepped down from the cross and saved yourself, but you went instead like a lamb to the slaughter, enduring death to bring us life. Forgive us for offering so little to you who gave so much. Amen.

113 You won't catch us following the crowd – that's what we tell ourselves, Lord – but we're wrong, aren't we, the pressure to conform or desire to keep up sometimes being hard to resist. Despite our best intentions, we go astray, time after time. Forgive us, and teach us to follow not the sheep but the shepherd. Amen.

114 Lord Jesus, thank you for giving your all, your blood poured out for us and for many on the cross so that we might taste the new wine of your love and never thirst again. Amen.

Easter

115 Risen Lord, may the wonder of this season point to a deeper wonder: your resurrection power that makes each day springtime, each moment a new dawn, full of promise. Help us to recognise that, with you, every apparent ending leads to a fresh start, death itself being the gate to life. Amen.

116 Living God, remind us that Jesus truly died, not just playing a part or going through the motions but enduring the darkness of death itself. Yet remind us also that he rose again, greeting his disciples in the upper room, meeting them on the road, restoring faith, hope, joy and purpose. So then, in the agony of bereavement, the trauma and despair of loss, assure us that beyond the grave lie new beginnings; that from dust and ashes you will bring new life that never ends. Amen.

117 Lord Jesus Christ, when shadows darken our lives and light seems suddenly extinguished, help us to remember that you endured death and rose victorious; that you experienced the full force of hatred and conquered it with love; that you took on the powers of evil and worked through them for good. Remind us, then, that your light will always shine, nothing in heaven or earth finally being able to overcome it. Amen.

118 Gracious God, save us from sentimentalising this season, settling for cosy pictures representing birth and new beginnings and forgetting what it cost you to bring us life. Remind us of how much you gave that we might receive, and help us to give something back in return, offering our love, our lives, our all to you. Amen.

119 Loving God, speak of your resurrection power through which your Son rose again and his followers bounced back from despair, and may that glorious message assure us that, however low life may bring us and however hard we fall, you will lift us up to new horizons, both now and for all eternity. Amen.

120 Lord of all, thank you that you do not leave us alone but instead draw alongside us through your Spirit. Thank you that, just as you met with your followers on the road and your disciples in the upper room, so, in Christ, you meet with us on the journey of life, always there, in your resurrection power, to guide, protect, comfort and support, each of us valued as a little child, chosen and precious to you. Amen.

121 Mighty God, remind us that though truth may be threatened by falsehood, good by evil, love by hatred and life by death, your purpose will always come through, nothing finally being allowed to frustrate your renewing power and redeeming grace. Amen.

122 Gracious God, speak through this day of birth and new life, of your Son rising from the tomb. Help us to greet this season with childlike enthusiasm, eager to celebrate what lies at its heart: your resurrection power and renewing love – good news today and every day. Amen.

123 Save us, Lord, from confusing the trappings of this season with its substance, from forgetting that the new beginnings they point to last not just for a season but for ever. Amen.

124 Mighty and mysterious God, though we struggle at times with the idea of resurrection, so much causing us to question, remind us of the way you changed the lives of the apostles and of countless others since, transforming doubt to faith, sorrow to joy and fear to confidence. Meet us, then, through the risen Christ, so that, incredible though it may seem, we may know him for ourselves, and share his life, now and for evermore. Amen.

125 Thank you, Lord, that the stone was rolled away and the grave empty; that your love conquered hatred, good vanquished evil, and life defeated death. Amen.

126 Eternal God, help us to celebrate life, and to rejoice in the beauty of this world, yet to remember always that this earthly body is only a shell, a pointer to what you yet hold in store. Amen.

127 Lord Jesus Christ, for your dying and rising again, your victory over darkness and death, we kneel before you in awe and worship, our Lord, and our God! Amen.

128 Thank you, Lord, that in the shadow of death, the darkness of the cross and the tomb, your love not only continued to shine, but burned more brightly than ever – life surrendered bringing the light of life to all. Amen.

129 Gracious God, speak afresh today of your love in Christ, his resurrection and the life you promise us in turn. Wherever we are, then, and whatever we do, help us to remember what this season is ultimately about and to make space for *you* as well as for us. Amen.

130 Lord Jesus, thank you that through your dying and rising among us what's done can be *un*done – mistakes forgiven and the past put behind us. Thank you that one thing alone can never be unravelled: your victory over sin and death. Amen.

131 Forgive us, Lord, for we pin our hopes on what can never satisfy – the rewards and riches of this world. Teach us, if we would put all our eggs in one basket, to let that basket be you. Amen.

Ascension Day

132 Saviour Christ, teach us to look for you on earth, instead of gazing up into heaven; to find you, the Lord of all, in those around us, the needs of the world, and the daily round of life. Amen.

133 Risen and exalted Lord, give us a sense of wonder in your presence, an appreciation of the privilege we have, day after day, moment by moment, of knowing you, the King of kings and Lord of lords, greater than words can express or the mind comprehend. Teach us to make time for you, not as an extra or afterthought but as our greatest joy and first priority, offering you our grateful praise and thankful service. Amen.

134 Almighty God, too easily, when it comes to faith, we settle for something less, our understanding of Christ being limited, partial – hidebound by narrow preconceptions and finite comprehension. Open our hearts to the full extent of his greatness, the wonder of who he is and all he has done, so that we may recognise the one made flesh as the living Word; the one who humbled himself on the cross as the risen Saviour, who lives and reigns with you, one God, now and always. Amen.

135 Lord Jesus Christ, whatever we call you, however much we honour your name, it can never be enough, never even begin to express the homage you are due, for you are higher than our highest thoughts, greater than the human mind can ever comprehend, worthy of all praise and adoration. Help us, today and always, to worship you as you deserve. Amen.

Pentecost

136 Gracious God, you call us to fruitful discipleship, to produce in our lives a harvest of your Spirit – love, joy, patience, kindness, generosity, faithfulness, gentleness and self-control – but, to our shame, the reality disappoints, the harvest we produce proving a travesty of what you hope to see. Have mercy, and, by your grace, nurture and nourish our faith, so that it may truly grow. Amen.

137 Eternal God, we find ourselves frequently tossed around by life, carried along by the wind of change, our convictions and principles blown about on the breeze like so much thistledown. Anchor us in your love, so that we may think, speak and act wisely, the course of our lives directed by the breath of your Spirit, and by that alone. Amen.

138 What harvest do we produce, Lord, if any at all? What fruits can be seen in our lives, testifying to the work of your Spirit, your presence within? We speak of love, joy, peace and gentleness – these to name but some – but so often the facts deny the theory, such fruits being conspicuously lacking. Reach out in mercy, and nurture the seeds you have sown within us, so that they may truly grow and flourish, to your glory. Amen.

139 Sovereign God, energise us by the breath of your Spirit, giving power for living through your love and goodness. Open our hearts to your presence flowing within, blowing away whatever keeps us from you, so that we may live and work more faithfully for your kingdom, this and every day. Amen.

140 Forgive us, Lord, for we don't produce what we should, too much in our lives being bad, too little proving good. Move within us through your Spirit, and make us fruitful for you. Amen.

141 Lord of all, too often we prevent your Spirit's power from getting through. We don't mean it to happen, and don't wilfully go wrong; it's just that we allow little things, small distractions, to come between us, inexorably multiplying, until we become detached from you, all contact broken, and the flow is stopped. Forgive us, restore the circuit, and connect us again. Amen.

142 Mighty God, may your Spirit course through us like a bubbling spring, a gushing fountain, a tranquil stream, a mighty river, bringing your love, joy, guidance and peace. So fill us with your presence that our souls may dance each day in jubilant praise and exultant gratitude. Amen.

143 Loving God, our faith is cloaked with cobwebs, having been left untouched too often and too long, neglected to the point of being redundant. We've been complacent, assuming discipleship can look after itself instead of needing a regular dusting down. Forgive us, and may your Spirit sweep through our lives, freshening up our faith and breathing new life within. Amen.

144 Refine us, redeemer God, through the flame of your Spirit, cleansing, purifying and recasting our lives. Come now with tongues of redeeming fire and create from what we are something new for you. Amen.

145 Spirit of God, remind us that we can no more fathom the workings of your mind than control the course of the wind; that we can never know, still less dictate, where and when you will move, or in what ways and among whom you may choose to act. Open our lives to whatever you would do, wherever, whenever and however you choose to do it. Amen.

Trinity Sunday

146 Almighty God, help us to see you in all your glory rather than in the single dimension we all too easily reduce you to. Help us to glimpse you as Father – providing, guiding, caring for us each day; to see you as Son – sharing our humanity and walking this earth; to experience you as Spirit – alive within, prompting, comforting, teaching and equipping. Give us a fuller picture of who and what you are, and an awareness that no dimension or measure can finally contain the wonder of it all. Amen.

147 Mighty and mysterious God, teach us that your ways are not our ways, nor your thoughts our thoughts; that, however much we understand of you, you will always be greater than we can fully grasp – known, yet beyond knowing. Amen.

148 Sovereign God, we can't explain it, how somehow you're both three persons yet one, but we know that we can relate to you in different ways: as Father, Son and Holy Spirit; Creator, Redeemer and Counsellor; a God above, alongside, yet within us, wonderful beyond words. Though that doesn't explain away the mystery, may it constantly remind us that knowing you involves a personal encounter and living experience, touching every part of who and what we are, each and every day. Amen.

All Saints' Day

149 Lord of past, present and future, inspire us through those rare people whose lives point to Christ, their thoughts, words and deeds speaking unanimously of him, their commitment clear, their faith unshakable and their love evident: an inspiration to subsequent generations. Help us to follow in their footsteps so that, despite our many faults, we may in some way rank among their number. Amen.

150 Eternal God, remind us of the great company of your people who have gone before us, famed or forgotten, celebrated or overlooked – all who have run their race and kept the faith, walking the way of Christ to their journey's end. Help us to learn from them, so that one day we too may perhaps give a lead, inspiring others to love and serve you in turn. Amen.

151 Lord Jesus Christ, thank you for those who have walked your way, leaving footsteps for us to follow. Whatever obstacles we may face, teach us to stay true to the path in turn, so that in some small way we may inspire others as they journey in faith. Amen.

Commitment

see also Discipleship, journey of; Growth in grace

152 Forgive us, Lord God, for imagining that discipleship can take care of itself; that we can sit back and expect faith to grow with no effort on our part. Teach us to work at our relationship with you, patiently and with diligence, so that you may bring the buds of commitment into full bloom, and our lives to true fruition. Amen.

153 Living God, give us genuine commitment in following you, wholehearted resolve to honour your will, sincere dedication in discipleship. Teach us truly to practise what we preach, in the sense of working at it each day until walking the way of Christ becomes second nature, not the exception but the norm. Amen.

154 Merciful God, though we speak of commitment, ours is a fair-weather discipleship, strong enough when the sun shines, but swift to founder should the wind blow cold. Forgive us, and grant us a faith for all seasons, as true to you in calm or storm as you are true to us. Amen.

155 Loving God, our faith blows hot and cold, sometimes setting us on fire with enthusiasm; at others, ardour cooled almost to zero; but more often – too often – we're lukewarm, little use to you or anyone. Kindle afresh a fire of devotion in our hearts, and fan there a burning desire to love and serve you better. Amen.

156 Eternal God, forgive us, for we grow stale sometimes, the freshness that marked our early years of faith becoming a distant memory, a shadow of what it once was and ought to be. Our spirit becomes shrivelled, hardened by exposure to the realities of life, and we grow set in our ways, closed to new ideas and experiences – closed to you. Where discipleship is desiccated and commitment withered, restore vitality, putting a new heart and right spirit within us. Amen.

157 Almighty God, keep us focused, single-minded in your service. Help us to fasten our eyes on you and your kingdom, and let nothing distract us from that end. Amen.

158 Lord Jesus Christ, forgive us, for we're careless in discipleship, reluctant to move away from the comfort zone. Forgive the complacency of our commitment, our doing as little rather than as much as possible, and teach us to offer instead not what we *must* but what we *may* do in your service, in glad and joyful response. Amen.

159 Sovereign God, we don't find immersing ourselves in faith easy. Though we talk blithely enough about it, when it comes to the moment of truth, to letting go and trusting you, we're as nervous as a kitten, testing the water but no more, and thus failing either to sink or swim. Give us the courage we need to take the plunge and place our all in your hands. Amen.

160 Eternal God, we like to think our commitment is permanent, strong and sure enough to last the test of time, but the truth is that, like so much else, it too can swiftly fade, losing its sheen as the years pass by. Disappointments, difficult demands, or simple complacency erode its vibrancy, until what's left is a pale shadow of what once was. Nourish our faith, restore and replenish it, so that it may be as real and fresh tomorrow as it is today, enduring untarnished to the end of time. Amen.

161 Gracious God we would consecrate ourselves to you as a fragrant offering, its scent pleasing in your eyes, its perfume carrying to others, speaking of your grace, goodness, purpose and love. Take our lives and transform them through your Spirit, so that who and what we are may reach up to you and out to all. Amen.

162 Gracious God, have mercy upon us, for we grow complacent in faith and lazy in discipleship, leaving to others what we should do ourselves. Teach us that commitment involves give as well as take, work for the body as well as rest for the soul. Amen.

163 Living God, give us a thirst for deeper faith – a resolve to grow in commitment, develop in understanding and mature in discipleship. Keep us young in spirit, childlike in our appetite for life and ever-youthful in our hunger to learn more of the world and more of you. Amen.

164 When opportunities present themselves, Lord – to love, serve and work for you – teach us to put aside any hesitations we may have, and to grasp the bull by the horns. Amen.

165 Redeemer God, deal graciously with us, for we put our hand to the plough, only to give up when the going proves tough. Help us to get the bit between our teeth once more, so that in due time you may reap a harvest. Amen.

166 Help us to honour you, Lord, not only in worship but above all in daily life – in our work and leisure, everything we do and are. Teach us to serve you not just on Sunday, but *every* day. Amen.

167 Mighty and marvellous God, when we were young in faith, we thought like children, spoke like children, acted like children, but you call us now to have moved on from childish things towards maturity in Christ. Save us from simply playing at discipleship, treating it as some kind of game or incidental pursuit. Help us to take commitment seriously, and make it for real. Amen.

168 Lord of all, it's easy to extol you in worship, much harder in the daily routine, but there too we need to recognise your presence and honour your call. However tedious or routine a task may be, help us to do it for you, consecrating even the most humdrum tasks of life to your glory. Amen.

169 Gracious God, have mercy on us, for we treat faith as an optional extra – something to put on when it suits us, and then leave off. Help us to commit ourselves wholeheartedly to you, lest we be more ornament than use. Amen.

170 Loving God, forgive our laziness in discipleship, our inclination to lounge in the comfort zone rather than stretch the muscles of faith. Forgive us for reducing what ought to be a way of life to a casual pursuit, a couch potato commitment that asks little and delivers less. Teach us to work at our faith, so that it not only shapes every aspect of life but is kept in shape in turn. Amen.

171 Lord Jesus Christ, when it comes to discipleship, for all our talk of commitment and sacrificial service we set our sights low, content to get by rather than excel. Forgive our limited aspirations and weakness of resolve, and help us to aim higher, targeting a deeper faith and fuller response to your love – a life more closely lived with you. Amen.

172 Sovereign God, remind us of the need to stay connected with you if our faith is to stay fresh and meaningful, able to meet the challenge of changing times. Teach us that it is not simply about a one-off commitment but about an ongoing relationship, the health of which depends on making time to hear your voice and discern your will. Put, then, your word on our tongue, your love in our heart, and your joy in our soul, this and every day. Amen.

173 Gracious God when it comes to serving you, you don't expect perfection, our lives, under your examination, invariably falling short. What you do ask is that we genuinely try to walk the way of Christ. Though we go on getting it wrong day after day, rarely even approaching the sort of standard we'd like, teach us never to lose heart or to stop striving to serve you better, for your love is as much for those who've tried and failed as for anyone else – perhaps for those most of all. Amen.

174 Loving God, you have shown us in Christ the way we ought to live, and we yearn to follow suit. But though the spirit's willing, the flesh is weak, the commitment we profess being found wanting when the chips are down. Forgive all that's lacking within us, and what we cannot do *alone*, help us to do with *you*. Amen.

175 Living God, teach us that, in life and in faith, we must plough our own furrow, not relying on anyone else, but making our own way, our own decisions. Help us to put in the time and effort needed to see lasting growth and a meaningful harvest, not just putting our hand to the plough but keeping it there, come what may. Amen.

176 Too often we leave things to you, Lord, expecting you to meet our every need. Teach us to play our part: to seek, that we may find. Amen.

177 Mighty God, we make excuses for our failure to serve you, claiming we've too much to do, that we're unsure of your will or that we lack the right gifts, but you know, as well as we do, that the reality is different: that more often than not we're just too lazy to be bothered. For our slothful commitment, our careless, casual discipleship, forgive us. Amen.

178 Eternal God, whatever else may seem like old hat, may the message of your love, your promise of new life, stay ever fresh, ever new. Amen.

179 When faith proves demanding, Lord, commitment involving cost, remind us that you call us not to a picnic, but to take up our cross and follow you. Amen.

Confession

see also Forgiveness; Grace of God; New beginnings

180 Merciful God, forgive us, for in all kinds of ways we dwell too much on ourselves: *our* interests, *our* ideas, *our* image. Save us from narrow introspection – a life that is so full of *us* that we lose sight of you and others. Instead of fretting over who and what we are, may our concern be to reflect you and you alone. Amen.

181 We've no problem saying sorry, Lord – at least, not with saying sorry to you – but unless our apologies are real, backed up by genuine remorse and a true desire to change, they mean nothing – all just empty words. Teach us not just to *say* sorry but to mean it. Amen.

182 Loving God, have mercy, for time and again we resist your will, preferring our way to yours. Forgive our rebellious spirit and teach us to work *with* you rather than *against*. Amen.

183 Lord Jesus Christ, forgive us for closing the door to you, repeatedly denying you access into our lives. Forgive us for shutting you out when your presence unsettles and your word confronts, when you ask questions of us we would rather not face and make demands we prefer to avoid. Open our hearts to your love, our minds to your truth and our souls to your grace, so that *you* might live in us and we in you. Amen.

184 Sovereign God, our faults seem small, barely worth bothering with sometimes, yet the consequences can be greater than we expect, an apparently trivial mistake having potentially devastating repercussions. However minor our weaknesses may be, teach us to consider where they might lead and to put things right before lasting damage is done. Amen.

185 Forgive us, Lord, for time and again we freeze you out of our lives, faith growing cold within us. Break the ice that comes between us, and thaw our frosty hearts. Amen.

186 Gracious God, there is so much rubbish in our lives, emotional baggage and mental clutter that we should have discarded long ago but that we've allowed to build up inside, suffocating, scarring, polluting, poisoning. Help us to recognise the litter that engulfs us, the dross that disfigures and despoils, and to dispose of it before it disposes of us. Amen.

187 Father God, have mercy, for we're prickly characters, easily needled. Help us, instead of taking offence, to recognise in ourselves the faults we're so swift to condemn in others. Amen.

188 Forgive us, Lord, for we've done wrong and are truly ashamed. Have mercy, and give us another chance. Amen.

189 Loving God, we treat you like a dispensing machine sometimes, as if all we have to do is press the right buttons and you will pander to our wishes. A drop of devotion and touch of faith, with a hint of penitence thrown in, and you're bound to come up with the goods, whatever we may ask. Forgive us for seeking to exploit rather than worship you, and teach us instead to focus on what we can give rather than on what we might receive. Amen.

190 Forgive us, Lord, for we grow blasé about what we know too well, dismissive of what's familiar. Teach us, as *you* do, to see the special in everyone and everything. Amen.

191 Holy and righteous God, purify us, for there is so much that sullies our lives. Purge us of all that muddies the waters, preventing us from being the people you would have us be. Draw us closer to you, so that your cleansing love may flow in and through us, and make us new. Amen.

192 Forgive us, Lord, for we cold-shoulder you sometimes, acting as though you're not even there. Though we ignore *you*, do not reject us. Amen.

193 Loving God, so easily we give the wrong message, little things in our lives, seemingly innocuous, denying rather than affirming you, obscuring your love instead of making it plain. Alert us to the way we can give mixed messages; to how thoughtless words and deeds, apparently trivial, can cause people to call into question or even reject the faith we proclaim. Help us to overcome our faults, lest they obscure the message of your love and lead others astray. Amen.

194 Lord Jesus Christ, we've done wrong, and there are no excuses. We've let you down, when we should have known better. Forgive us, for we're truly sorry, more than words can say. Amen.

195 Gracious God, teach us to confess our sins to you instead of struggling with guilt or hiding away in fear. Help us to let go of the burden, knowing that you seek to pardon rather than condemn, bless instead of punish. Give us courage to openly and honestly acknowledge our faults so that we may find the freedom you alone can give. Amen.

196 Loving God, too much contaminates our lives – impure thoughts, foolish words and thoughtless actions; a host of attitudes, desires, weaknesses and faults that pollute and destroy. And, hard though we try, we cannot rid ourselves of them, their hold on us being too great. Reach out in mercy, and cleanse us of all that undermines our inner health, so that, by your love, we may be truly whole. Amen.

197 Forgive us, Lord, for we've done wrong, letting you down once again. We didn't mean to, *truly*, and we're ashamed, more sorry than words can say. Have mercy, and give us another chance. Amen.

Contentment

198 Generous God, remind us, when we feel hard done by, of all we have received, the many reasons we have to be thankful. Instead of envying those with more, teach us to remember those with so much less and gratefully to share from our plenty. Amen.

199 Eternal God, so much that we look forward to, fails to deliver, exposed as empty froth after the bubble bursts. Hopes fall short of expectations, promise proves short-lived. Thank you that the blessings of your kingdom are different, satisfying beyond measure – joy that never fades, love that never fails, life that never ends. Amen.

200 Almighty God, forgive us, for you promise us treasure in heaven yet we're irresistibly drawn by trinkets on earth. Instead of seeking the things of your kingdom, we neglect what's of real value, focusing instead on gathering worthless possessions. Teach us again where true riches lie, and help us to pursue them alone. Amen.

201 Guide us, Lord, for we hop from one thing to another, constantly searching for joy and fulfilment. Help us to take the leap of faith and find contentment in you. Amen.

202 Loving God, help us to be content, secure in who and what we are, assured that, despite our imperfections, you treasure us as your own. Amen.

203 Merciful God, forgive us, for instead of celebrating the good things you've given, we brood over what we're lacking and complain about our lot. Save us from ungratefulness, lest we bite the hand that feeds us. Amen.

204 Lord of all, in so much of life we hold on to things we don't need, believing they're essential and reluctant to let them go. We cling to money, possessions, hopes, memories; and we store up grievances, hurt and resentment, unable to forgive and forget. Instead of celebrating the freedom you offer we limp through life struggling with heavy burdens. Teach us to lay aside the weights that hold us down, and to travel light along the way of Christ. Amen.

205 Instead of ceaselessly striving, brooding about problems or dwelling on disappointments, teach us, Lord, to count our blessings and to be truly content. Amen.

206 Gracious God, time and again we foolishly imagine that the grass is greener on the other side, envying others as a result before finally discovering we were wrong. Forgive us, and teach us to appreciate what we have, while we still have it. Amen.

207 Mighty God, it's hard to resist, the promise of immediate pleasure, instant gratification, but you offer eternal sustenance, nourishing deep within. Teach us to feed on what truly satisfies, nourishing deep within; to taste of your love and know that it is good. Teach us, above all things, to hunger for you. Amen.

208 Living God, we thirst for many things in life, some more than others – luxury, riches and success among them – but few live up to expectations, still less fully satisfy. Teach us to drink of living water, the new wine you offer in Christ, and never to thirst again. Amen.

209 Forgive us, Lord, for we spend so long yearning for what we haven't got instead of celebrating what we have. Teach us to appreciate our many blessings and not to begrudge others theirs. Amen.

210 Living God, guide us, for we waste so much of our lives on a wild goose chase, seeking contentment where it cannot be found. Teach us to look to you, in whom alone is true joy and lasting fulfilment. Amen.

211 Gracious God we have so much to celebrate, yet instead of rejoicing in all you have given, the countless blessings you so freely shower upon us, we brood over disappointments, fret about the future, complain about our lot and dwell on our troubles until we can no longer see beyond them, our spirit closed to the generosity of your provision. Forgive us, and teach us each day to exult in your awesome gift of life, now and for all eternity. Amen.

212 Merciful God, forgive us, for too often we treat you like some kind of heavenly tap, expecting you to supply whatever we want, whenever we want it – blessings on demand. Remind us that you *do* provide – more than we can ever ask for – but not necessarily the things of this world, your gifts being of a different kind, nurturing the spirit and enriching within. Teach us to thirst for such things – gifts of your kingdom – and to be truly satisfied. Amen.

213 Help us, Lord, for so often we attempt to grab happiness only to find ourselves clutching at thin air. Teach us to reach out to you, and find true contentment. Amen.

214 Living God, we mean to focus on treasures in heaven, but the lure of earthly goods is so strong that we buy first this, then that, until shelves groan and cupboards creak under their weight, and the irony is that our possessions hang heavily on us too, becoming a burden rather than blessing, encumbrance rather than asset Teach us to let go of the clutter that ties us to earth, so that our spirits might soar unfettered, truly free. Amen.

215 We should be content, Lord, but instead of counting our blessings we dwell on what's still not ours. Forgive us and teach us to be satisfied with what we have. Amen.

216 Eternal God, remind us, should we ever forget it, that goods and possessions may feed the body but not the soul, delight the senses but not the spirit – contentment being a gift rather than a product, a treasure to be received rather than commodity plucked from a shelf. Teach us where true fulfilment lies, and to seek it before all else. Amen.

217 Lord Jesus Christ, forgive us, for we're drawn by show rather than substance, by glitz and trivia rather than what truly satisfies. Save us from swapping treasure in heaven for trinkets on earth. Amen.

218 Loving God, so much in life is special when enjoyed in moderation, but we indulge to excess, time and again craving that little bit more, rarely content with what we have. Remind us that we can all have too much of a good thing, and help us to recognise when enough is enough. Amen.

219 Eternal God, remind us that nothing in life lasts for ever, the world's beauty, joy and pleasure, special though they are, being all too fleeting, ours but for a moment. Help us, then, to celebrate such gifts, but never to pin our happiness upon them, seeking rather treasure in heaven, your kingdom that will neither fade nor perish. Amen.

220 Generous God, thank you for nourishing our soul – for offering us not just scraps from under your table, but the finest of food, eternal sustenance, satisfying deep within. Amen.

221 Loving Lord, we know it's foolish to assume that the grass is greener on the other side; to covet what we do not have and hanker after what we cannot reach, as though we're somehow missing out on what others around us enjoy; yet we do it all the time. Teach us, instead, to count our blessings, more than we can number, and to be content. Amen.

222 Gracious God, we can buy *most* things, but not *all* – not those that really matter, able to satisfy the soul rather than body. Only you can provide such things, through Christ offering true and lasting fulfilment. Teach us, in this materialist consumer world, never to lose sight of the blessings you offer – love, joy, hope and peace – gifts beyond price. Amen.

223 Too easily, Lord, we make riches our goal and possessions our god, only to end up the poorer. Remind us that money can buy much, but not happiness. Amen.

224 Everlasting God, so much that we pin our hopes on turns out to be empty, failing to bring the happiness we expected. Teach us to receive your gift of life, able to meet our deepest needs and satisfy beyond measure. Amen.

225 Living Lord, we don't think of ourselves as gluttonous, but we are just that sometimes, eating far more than we need while others go hungry. Help us to recognise when enough is enough and, instead of overfeeding ourselves, to think of those not fed at all. Amen.

226 We're sorry, Lord, for we hoard up worthless trinkets, neglecting what's of real value: treasure in heaven. Remind us that not all that glistens is gold. Amen.

Discipleship, journey of

see also Commitment; Growth in grace; Guidance

227 Almighty God, are we ready for the journey of faith? Are the mechanics of discipleship in place, the nuts and bolts of faith firmly secured? We like to think so, but we rarely take time to check, assuming instead that everything will take care of itself. Test us and correct our faults, examine us and tune our will to yours, so that, however demanding the road, we may travel it safely with you until our journey's end. Amen.

228 Lord Jesus Christ, save us from cautious discipleship, a faith that is afraid to take risks. Help us to recognise that what we cannot do alone is more than possible with you. Teach us, then, to recognise and grasp the opportunities you provide for service, witness and growth in grace. However tempting it may be to hold on to what is reassuringly familiar, give us the courage we need to step out into the unknown, exploring new horizons, new experiences of your love. Amen.

229 Living God, for us all life brings its ups and downs, highs and lows, peaks and troughs. Remind us that those belong together, each a part of the greater whole, and teach us to trust you come what may, sensing through them all the rhythm of your grace and heartbeat of your love. Amen.

230 Help us to walk your way, Lord; to match our steps to yours. Wherever you lead, teach us to follow. Amen.

231 Loving God, save us from becoming creatures of habit, expecting the same old thing out of discipleship and reducing it to a monotonous routine. Open our mind to new horizons, new experiences, new possibilities – to the continuing adventure of faith. Amen.

232 Lord Jesus Christ, it feels easy at first, walking your way – the path seeming clear, the journey simple – but slowly the going gets harder, the trail obscure, until finally we can end up losing heart and turning back, preferring the wide and inviting way of the world, which promises much and asks little, to the demanding path of service. Yet though that route seems easier, it leads to nowhere. Guide our footsteps and give us strength to finish the journey of discipleship, however challenging the course may be. Amen.

233 Eternal God, our human span, like the flower of the field's, is all too brief, in the context of the universe just a passing moment, a fleeting shadow. Help us to make the most of the time you give us, living each moment to the full and, in our own small way, reflecting something of your love and glory, until that day when we do not merely *glimpse* paradise but behold it in all its glory. Amen.

234 Gracious God, teach us to recall the past but not cling to it, to understand that life must be lived forwards rather than backwards, what *has been* representing simply a stepping stone to what is *yet to be*. Amen.

235 Eternal God, we try to walk the way of Christ, but we repeatedly slip up, temptation and weakness causing us to founder, and before we know it we find ourselves back where we started, the journey of discipleship proving more demanding than we ever imagined. Guide our footsteps, so that we may tread the path of faith more surely. And should we slide backwards, take us by the hand and lead us forward again. Amen.

236 Sovereign God, remind us that discipleship is a journey, not a destination; that it's about moving forward: exploring fresh horizons, discovering new possibilities and experiencing yet more of your love. Save us from getting stuck in a spiritual rut, settling for what is comfortable and familiar. Teach us, instead, to let go of whatever holds us back and to venture out in faith, open to whatever you hold in store. Amen.

237 Caring and compassionate God, thank you that, in the journey of life, you are always there beside us, to support and strengthen, to share the load, to help us through when we feel unable to cope. Though we struggle to learn, instruct, control and direct us, so that *your* will may become our will, and our way, your way. Amen.

238 Living God, though routine is part of life, unwelcome but unavoidable, may our love for you stay fresh and full of promise. Instead of discipleship becoming mere habit, reduced to empty repetition, keep it alive, vibrant, sparkling – a continuing journey of discovery in which what is old is ever new. Amen.

239 Lord Jesus Christ, remind us that you call us not simply to a destination, but also to a journey, a daily adventure with you. Amen.

240 Loving God, though there's no simple tool for assessing the state of our faith, help us to gauge our spiritual progress, recognising how far we've come and how far we've yet to go. Save us from going back over the same old ground and settling for the familiar and undemanding, but save us also from getting ahead of ourselves, believing that the tale is complete when it's barely started. Show us where we are and where you would have us be, and, as we work at the task of discipleship, help us to advance, stage by stage, to a deeper knowledge of you. Amen.

241 Mighty God, we like to think our faith is impregnable, able to stand up to whatever life may throw against it. But we know it's not, for – remorselessly attacked – it's imperceptibly eroded over the years. Though the assault may be subtle, often passing unnoticed, the temptation to compromise is always there – insidiously gnawing away at our commitment, until it's a shadow of what it used to be. Strengthen our faith, that it may stand the passage of time, as real tomorrow as it is today. Amen.

242 Lord Jesus Christ, we talk of discipleship as a stiff test, demanding examination, perseverance, if we're to finish the course – but does the practice match the theory; does commitment, in reality, ask anything of us at all? Forgive us, for our words say one thing but our deeds another, the faith we settle for rarely making demands on the way we live, still less taking as much out of us as it puts in. Teach us truly to follow, truly to serve, so that we may not just *talk* of discipleship but know we've run the race. Amen.

243 Save us, Lord, from thinking we've arrived as Christians. Remind us that faith is a continuing journey, our destination being not on earth but in heaven. Amen.

244 Whatever hurdles obstruct our faith, Lord – hindering us from loving you, preventing us from knowing you, impeding us from serving you – help us to surmount them all. Amen.

245 Almighty God, when we're drained by the rat-race of life, wearied by its ceaseless demands, renew our strength, and help us to go the extra mile. However tough the challenge may be, however demanding the course, give us the help we need to meet it. Amen.

246 You call us to a journey of faith, Lord, venturing out into the unknown. Help us to respond to your still small voice within, and to follow where you lead. Amen.

Faithfulness of God

see also Hope and trust

247 Eternal God, forgive us, for we forget you too easily, your many gifts and countless promises slipping from our minds. Slow to recall your faithfulness across the years, we fail to make time for you as we should, overlooking your awesome goodness and taking your love for granted. Remind us of all you are, all you have done and all you are doing, and keep such knowledge fresh in our minds, each moment of every day. Amen.

248 Our cup may be small, Lord, but it's sufficient for all our needs. For your faithful provision, day after day, thank you. Amen.

249 God of past, present and future, only *you* do not change. Your love is eternal, your mercy constant, your purpose enduring. Teach us in this shifting world, here today and gone tomorrow, to trust in you, the same now and always. Amen.

250 Eternal God, so much in life drifts away like thistledown on the breeze. Remind us that your love alone endures for ever; the same yesterday, today and tomorrow. Amen.

251 Almighty God, thank you for guarding us, faithfully providing shelter and protection when storms brew and waves threaten to sweep us away. Thank you for the strength of your love and certainty of your promise, the knowledge that though all else may pass away your goodness will continue, solid and secure in an ever-changing universe. Whatever we face, we will not fear, for you are with us, the same yesterday, today and for ever. Amen.

252 God of space and time, before all and beyond all, remind us that your word is constant, your promise sure, your faithfulness certain. Though all else may disappoint, remind us that you will not. Amen.

253 Living God, our hold on life is vulnerable, the happiness we find and goals we strive for being like sandcastles on the beach, destined to be destroyed by the in-rushing tide. So much in this world is shifting or easily undermined, here today and gone tomorrow. Teach us to build wisely, seeking fulfilment in your love, which, alone, is able to face the restless waves and still stand firm for ever. Amen.

254 Gracious God, thank you for the relationship we enjoy with you – your faithfulness across the years, your enduring love, your companionship through the journey of life – and forgive us that all too often it has been one-sided, you having to do all the running. Renew our commitment and deepen our devotion, so that we may respond in kind, offering something back to you who has done so much for us. Amen.

255 Creator God, thank you for your faithful provision and constant love. Through sunshine and storm, summer or winter, it remains the same – a stream of living water, refreshing and reviving, unfailing come what may. For the constancy of that provision, receive our praise. Amen.

256 Though our resources fail, Lord, and though others let us down, teach us that, no matter what, we can count on you. Amen.

257 Eternal God, thank you that, though heaven and earth pass away, your love endures for ever; that, in a world of change, you are our rock – solid ground beneath our feet. Amen.

258 Gracious God, we're forgetful of you much of the time, paying you scant heed until trouble strikes, only then remembering your love and running for shelter in your protective arms – a refuge in time of need. Yet, though we ignore you for so long, always you are ready to welcome, as faithful as we are fickle. Thank you for being there, come rain or shine. Amen.

259 Living God, we assume sometimes that our happiness is secure, solid, but it's not, for it is so easily punctured, few things being as permanent as they seem. Teach us to trust in you, knowing that though all else may fail, *you* will not. Amen.

260 Loving God, when we feel lost, isolated, abandoned, remind us that we're not alone – that, however distant you may seem, you are here by our side. Amen.

261 Eternal God, you never tire or slumber. Your love is constant each day, your faithfulness ever sure. Whatever we face, you are there watching over us – guiding, protecting, loving, forgiving – your goodness never exhausted, your compassion never failing. For that assurance, receive our praise. Amen.

262 Loving God, you watch over us, hour after hour, day after day, not to keep tabs on what we are doing but as a loving friend and faithful companion – there to help in times of need, protect in times of danger and comfort in times of hurt. Thank you for the knowledge that, though we lose sight of *you*, still *you* look out for us. Amen.

263 Merciful God, your love wells up, sparkling and irrepressible, day upon day, year upon year, an unfailing spring of living water, poured out beyond our deserving so that our cup overflows. For your faithful blessing, so freely given, so joyfully received, receive our praise. Amen.

264 Thank you, Lord, that what you have promised to do, will be done; that when you give your word, you will always honour it. Amen.

265 Everlasting God, wherever we may be, whatever life may bring, you are our shelter, our eternal home. Amen.

Father's Day

266 Father God, for your awesome love, faithful care, patient guidance and constant support, thank you. Amen.

267 Father of all, help us to show our love for you, not through sophisticated language or polished prayers but through true commitment, responding with childlike trust, gratitude and affection to your fatherly care. Teach us to open our hearts to you, as you have so freely done to us. Amen.

268 Father God, thank you, for you have given us life and called us your children. Nurture us, and help us to grow. Amen.

Fellowship

269 Lord of all, remind us that we need others as they need us; that you call us not to isolated commitment but to a community of faith, working with others to make possible what we could never achieve alone. Amen.

270 Living God, teach us in the marathon journey of faith that we run not *against* others but *with* them, part of the great company of your people, sharing a common cause and seeking the same goal. For the solidarity this brings, the support and encouragement both given and received, receive our thanks. Amen.

271 Loving God, thank you for the companionship of others – the way family, friends, colleagues and acquaintances all contribute to our lives, helping to shape us as people. Thank you, above all, for the fellowship of the Church – for calling us into a community of faith, your family, in order that there too we might give and receive. Open our eyes to everything we can learn from others – the support, enrichment and understanding they can offer – and to all that we can do for them in turn. Remind us that we're called not just to individual discipleship but also to shared commitment; that if we're to serve you effectively, and help others to do the same, *we* need them and *they* need us. Amen.

Forgiveness

see also Confession; Grace of God; New beginnings

272 Gracious God, thank you that you keep no record of wrongs, no track of our mistakes, always being ready instead to wipe the slate clean and put the past behind us. Though we are guilty according to the law, thank you for acquitting us by your grace; the debt paid, sins forgiven and forgotten. Amen.

273 Merciful God, forgive us, for instead of confessing our mistakes and receiving forgiveness we try to hide them, digging ourselves into an ever-deeper hole. Teach us to acknowledge our faults before they bury us completely. Amen.

274 Redeemer God, remind us that though our sins are as scarlet, they shall be white as snow; that your love is able to cover over all our faults, transforming what is and shaping what shall be. Amen.

275 Gracious God, we need to be disciplined sometimes, unwelcome though it might be. We have to learn to face up to the consequences of our actions, pay the price of some folly, learn our lesson, pay our dues. We don't enjoy it any more than the next person, but help us at such times to remember it's for our own good, the prescription designed to heal, not hurt, correct rather than castigate, discipline instead of punish. Though we do not relish the treatment, use it to make us whole. Amen.

276 Thank you, Lord, that when we get things wrong you don't put us in a corner, holding us up to disgrace. Always you forgive and forget, helping us to start again. Amen.

277 Loving God, there are countless faults in our lives, and we try vainly to whitewash over them, hiding them from view. But only *you* can do that, your love covering what we can never hope to conceal. Come now, and though our sins are as scarlet, make us whiter than snow. Amen.

278 Merciful God, past mistakes and present faults stick to us like grime and, try though we might, we cannot remove them. Wash us, for you alone can make us clean. Amen.

279 Though we hide from you, Lord, you see us as we are, nothing being concealed from your gaze. Teach us, then, to face you openly, knowing that, whatever we have done, you delight to forgive and forget. Amen.

280 Gracious God, thank you that you keep no record of wrongs, no track of mistakes, always looking instead to forgive and forget. Save us from dwelling on what's already dealt with, from playing over and over again what your love has wiped clean. Amen.

281 Merciful God, we can pull the wool over some people's eyes – even our own – but *you* see and know us as we really are. Teach us, then, to acknowledge our mistakes and to trust in your forgiveness. Amen.

282 Loving God, though we make our own bed in life, thank you that we don't have to lie on it, despite what the world may say. Thank you that it is never too late to make up for our mistakes, your grace offering us the chance to start again, doing today what we should have done before. Amen.

283 Redeemer God, we look to you, wide-eyed with wonder, for though we repeatedly flout your will, disobeying your commands, always you forgive us, nothing able to exhaust your patience or deny your love. Amen.

284 Gracious God, you have cause to punish, more grounds for passing sentence than any, for we repeatedly flout your will and disobey your commandments, but your nature is always to pardon. Instead of holding our faults against us, you offer full and free forgiveness, the opportunity to start again. For the wonder of your mercy, we thank you. Amen.

285 Holy and righteous God, though we wish it were otherwise, we know that sometimes, for our own good, we must take our medicine. If we're to learn from our mistakes, deal with the consequences of our actions, and grow healthier in discipleship, then we must accept the remedy you prescribe, however unwelcome it may be. Reach out in love, and make us whole. Amen.

Freedom in Christ

see also Intercession: For those who feel trapped

286 Liberating God, thank you, for we were held captive, imprisoned by fear, doubt, darkness and death, and through your dying and rising again you have set us free. Amen.

287 Loving God, forgive us, for we fritter away the freedom you offer, erecting fresh barriers of weakness and disobedience as fast as you pull them down. Release us from all that holds us captive, and open our hearts to your gift of life. Amen.

288 Thank you, Lord, for our spirit was chained, shackled to this world, but you gave us wings, and set us free. Amen.

289 Loving God, we can feel trapped sometimes, the bars of fear proving as impregnable as any prison, of insecurity as any cell, of prejudice as any jail, of self as any dungeon. Unlock the door and break our bonds, so that we might be truly free. Amen.

Gifts, using

290 Almighty God, however small we are, however insignificant we may consider ourselves compared to others, teach us that with your help we can do surprising things, greater than we would believe possible. Teach us to recognise the abilities you have given, and to use them to the full. Amen.

291 Lord of all, whatever sphere of service you call us to, whether in the limelight or behind the scenes, making a splash or passing unnoticed, help us to do it to the best of our ability. Equip us to play our part faithfully in the grand scheme of your purpose, and to recognise equally the contribution made by others, understanding that there are many ways of working for your kingdom, each equally important. Teach us, then, to offer our gifts, our work, our lives to you, serving whenever and wherever we can. Amen.

292 Loving God, our gifts aren't eye-catching, never destined to turn heads or win plaudits, but they're gifts nonetheless, held in trust for you. Help us to make the most of them, and to use them not just for our benefit but for that of others too, consecrating all we are and all we do to your service. Amen.

293 Living God, we have our aspirations, all kinds of high ambitions, but we know too, in our heart of hearts, that not all our goals can be realised. Help us to recognise what we *can* do and what we *can't*, and, wherever possible, may we use the gifts you've given in your service. Amen.

294 When we're tempted, Lord, to bite off more than we can chew, to take on what's clearly beyond us, teach us to think again. Help us to recognise our gifts, but also our limitations. Amen.

Giving, to others

see also Grace before meals; Intercession: For the poor and hungry

295 Save us, Lord, from a mean, acquisitive spirit. Instead of hoarding up treasure for ourselves, help us to give – to you, and to others. Amen.

296 Merciful God, forgive us, for we have received so much yet give so little, frittering away money on trivia and luxuries we do not need, while a multitude suffer and die for want of a pittance. Remind us of how fortunate we are and of all we can do for others at such minimal cost, and teach us to respond, ready to give not just our small change, but sacrificially, just as you gave your all for us. Amen.

297 Have we done enough, Lord? We've given, certainly, but was each donation a meaningful gift or a token gesture, a response from the heart or an attempt to salve our conscience? We've offered a little but not much, what we spare for others over a lifetime barely being what we spend on ourselves in a week. Forgive us, and teach us to deal generously, as you have dealt generously with us. Amen.

298 Loving God, forgive us, for we spend more on one treat for ourselves than on what we give to others. We extol the virtue of a generous heart yet display the meanest of spirits, our talk of concern and compassion repeatedly being exposed for the sham it is. Teach us, next time we're asked to give, to respond gladly, and to offer not the least we can get away with but more than we can truly afford. Amen.

299 Lord of all, so many in this world simply *survive*, struggling each day to get by as best they can. Not for them the trappings of life we take for granted, the accoutrements we see as ours by right. They are happy to find even the bare essentials, let alone more. Help us to remember how lucky we are, how much we have to celebrate, and teach us to respond, generously and lovingly, so that others may rejoice in turn. Amen.

300 Gracious God, teach us how lucky we are compared to millions across the world; so many having barely enough to exist, let alone the good things we take for granted. Teach us to focus on their *needs* rather than our *extras* and to realise that through giving a little we can bring them *much*. Amen.

301 We don't earn much, Lord – a mere pittance compared to some – but it's a king's ransom to others, riches beyond their wildest dreams. However much then we may strive for more, teach us first to appreciate what we have, and gratefully to respond to those with so much less. Amen.

302 Lord of all, we're not as mean as some, or at least we hope we're not, but we're not as generous as we could be either, money being more important to us than it should be, and more of a driving force in our lives than we like to think. Teach us to steward it wisely, but equally to give it freely, lest what we possess ends up possessing us. Amen.

303 Loving God, give us generosity of heart and kindliness of spirit, so that instead of hoarding good things for ourselves, we may share them with others, as you have shared so much with us. Amen.

Glory of God, glimpsing

see also Greatness of God; Power of God

304 Mighty and mysterious God, before you we must turn aside, your splendour being too intense, your brightness too awesome, and yet, through Christ, we glimpse your grace and glory, wonderful beyond words. For the present it is partial, as though we look through darkened glasses, but it is enough and more than enough to lighten our path and illuminate our soul. Shine now, shine always, through his radiant love. Amen.

305 Creator God, forgive us, for we see some things so often that we lose sight of their beauty, foolishly dismissing them as ordinary. Help us to see the unique in the familiar, the special in the everyday. Amen.

306 Almighty God, give us a sense of awe in your presence, a deeper understanding of your greatness and grandeur. Help us, each day, to glimpse your glory more clearly, so that, marvelling at who and what you are, we may respond in reverent praise and joyful worship. Amen.

307 Sovereign God, give wings to our souls so that, though we're tied in body to earth, we may rise to you in spirit, our perception of things below being transformed by your kingdom above. Help us to see beyond the horizons of this world to what can and shall be, by your grace and through your power. Amen.

308 Mighty God, help us, for in all kinds of ways we become short-sighted, having eyes only for what we want to see. Preoccupied with self, we struggle to look beyond our narrow horizons to the bigger picture. Help us to focus each day on who and what you are, and so to live each day in the context of your love, your call, your will and your word. Help us to glimpse you in all your glory. Amen.

309 Gracious God, release us from the chains that shackle us to this world, encumbering our mind and imprisoning our spirit. Grant us a deeper knowledge of the truth that sets us free, so that we might rise on wings of faith and soar in the light of your love, celebrating the glorious liberty your grace bestows and glimpsing a little more of your glory. Amen.

310 Sovereign God, set our hearts on things above but keep our faith firmly on the ground, relevant to daily life, shaping the things we think and say and do. Touch the ordinary with the wonder of your presence, so that each moment may speak of you and be lived in the light of your love. Amen.

311 Creator God, the vastness of space leaves us reeling, such magnitude truly awesome, yet you brought it all into being, sustaining it each day and leading it towards fulfilment; the universe and everything within it being the work of your hands. As you created the stars and the sand, so you have fashioned our lives – knowing us better than we know ourselves, calling us by name, loving us more than we can begin to fathom. For the vastness of your purpose, the immensity of your creation and the mind-boggling wonder of your grace, thank you. Amen.

312 Gracious God, we've hopefully grasped at least something about you – the breadth of your love, extent of your mercy, power of your word and scope of your purpose – but save us from imagining we know it all, that we've even begun to fathom, let alone exhaust, the infinite riches of who and what you are. Whatever we've experienced, teach us that there is far more still to be explored – enough for *this* life and beyond. Amen.

313 Eternal God, when it comes to you and the things of your kingdom, we glimpse only the vaguest outline of reality, a mere fraction of the truth, yet we confuse this partial picture with the full vista, imagining we have seen all we need to see. Forgive us, and open our eyes to the wonder of your presence, the fullness of your truth, the richness of your love and the immensity of your purpose. Amen.

314 Mighty God, may knowing you cause us to catch our breath in wonder, to exult and marvel. Instead of being an arid issue of the mind – an intellectual assent to truth – may faith be an affair of the heart, capturing our imagination and transporting us into your presence, so that, overwhelmed with joy and filled with awe, our spirit may rise to you each day in rapturous praise and grateful worship. Amen.

315 Creator God, teach us to glimpse you in the daily round of life and the wonder of this world. Where others look and see nothing, help us to observe with the eye of faith, perceiving the reality beneath the surface. Open our hearts as well as our eyes, so that we may look and truly see. Amen.

316 Thank you, Lord, for making the ordinary special, the everyday unique, the simple profound – so much in life speaking of you. Amen.

317 Awesome God, you lift our thoughts to things above, offering a glimpse of your presence, a taste of your kingdom, and our hearts soar to you in joy and wonder. Thank you for who and what you are. Amen.

318 Living God, there are times when our wings need clipping in order to take us down a bit – but save us from becoming so tied to this world that we are unable to rise above the petty and mundane. Liberate our spirit, so that we may climb to you on eagle's wings, catching a vision of what life can be, what we can do and what you are doing – a glimpse of the special in the ordinary, the sacred in the secular, the divine in the daily round of life. Amen.

319 Mighty and mysterious God, thank you that though we but glimpse you now, our understanding being partial and our faith flawed, one day we will see you face to face and know you fully, even as you know us. Amen.

320 Sovereign God, there's so much we don't see, the world of our senses not representing the whole story but giving just a glimpse of reality, one aspect of a greater whole. Save us from being bound by our limited horizons, closing our lives to wonders beyond and riches yet to be revealed. Open our hearts to your infinite love, greater than eye has seen or mind conceived. Amen.

321 Living God, wipe clear the windows of our souls, so that, seeing you better, we may know you more fully. Grant us a clearer picture of you that sheds new light on every aspect of life, every part transformed by your sanctifying touch. Amen.

Grace before meals

322 In a world of hunger, Lord, teach us to appreciate our plenty and to share it with those whose plate is empty. Remind us of how lucky we are and help us never to forget those less fortunate. May our gratitude to you spill over in generosity towards all. Amen.

323 Gracious God, we've enough and more than enough, your love showering us with good things, too many to number. Teach us to remember those with so much less. Amen.

324 Lord of all, whenever we eat, teach us to pause for a moment, to think of others, and to realise how lucky we are. Amen.

325 In a world of limited resources, Lord, where a few have too much and most have too little, teach us there's enough for all, if we can only learn to share. Amen.

326 Generous God, you have prepared a table for us spread with good things, the finest of fare. Teach us to share our plenty with others, as you have shared with us. Amen.

327 Lord of all, in a world of hunger, where so many find their plate empty, teach us to appreciate the many good things we have and to share freely, love widely and give generously. Amen.

328 Forgive us, Lord, for we feast while others starve, our plenty being bought at their cost. Instead of a hunger for more, give us a hunger for justice. Amen.

329 Loving God, in a world of rich and poor, plenty and privation, teach us to have enough, but not too much. Amen.

330 Teach us, Lord, in our plenty, to remember those with so much less, for should we forget them, we forget you too. Amen.

Grace of God

see also Confession; Forgiveness; Love, of God; New beginnings

331 Thank you, Lord, for you have blessed us, more than we deserve, more than we could ask, more than we ever dreamt possible! Amen.

332 Loving God, how would we fare, were our lives to be scrutinised, assessed, weighed in the balance? Would we come up to scratch, pass muster as a follower of Christ? We fear not, for there's so much wrong in our lives, so many ways we fall short. Yet the mystery is that you *do* examine us, searching our hearts and weighing the spirit, and though we fail on innumerable counts, *still* you accept us as we are; enough to call us your children. For that awesome, astonishing truth, we thank you. Amen.

333 Merciful God, thank you for the contract you have made in Christ, the new covenant sealed by his death and resurrection, offering new life and love to all. Thank you that all it asks for is a response in faith – no signing on the dotted line or assent to complex formulae, but a simple act of commitment. Above all, thank you for honouring your pledge, keeping to your side of the bargain even though we repeatedly renege on ours. Amen.

334 Generous God, thank you, for though we deserve so little, you give us so much, filling our lives with good things, too many to number. Amen.

335 Gracious God, though we know we shouldn't, we still perceive you as a setter of rules: he who must be obeyed. Teach us that you are not always looking over our shoulder, waiting to trip us up, but that you stand by our side, constantly ready to affirm and encourage, inviting us to share your life and be truly free. Amen.

336 Redeemer God, for your cleansing love and constant care, washing away the dirt from our lives and making us new, thank you. For pouring out your blessings, day after day showering us with good things, receive our grateful praise. Amen.

337 Living God, we can never earn your love, still less repay your goodness towards us, but you do not ask us to. You have cancelled the debt, writing it off as though it had never been. Though we owe so much, you ask us simply to receive. Though we deserve so little, you offer new life in Christ, free and overflowing. For the awesome generosity of your gift, we thank you. Amen.

338 Merciful God, thank you for offering us your love, your joy, your peace and your mercy. Thank you that these are no stunt, but truly free to all, needing us only to reach out and receive. For the awesome gift of your Son and all that it means, receive our praise. Amen.

339 Gracious God, you set us rules to live by, and we don't always like obeying them – not when they clash with personal gratification or demand more of us than we'd like to give – yet you impose them for our benefit rather than yours, so that all can enjoy your blessings and live life to the full. Teach us, then, not to fear you as one rigidly imposing law but, freely, gladly and gratefully, to honour your will. Amen.

340 Thank you, Lord, that though our faith grows cold, your love stays warm; that though we freeze you out, you melt our frosty heart. Amen.

341 Loving God, you could easily and fairly reject us, for we fall short in so many ways of the people we ought to be. Yet, for all our faults, you refuse to let us go, counting us of inestimable value, and working tirelessly to make us new. For that patient and faithful love, thank you. Amen.

342 Gracious God, thank you that we can meet your gaze, not with fear but with faith, for you look on us with love and compassion, seeking to heal rather than harm, help instead of hurt. Thank you that we can look you in the eye with confidence, assured that, despite our faults, weaknesses and disobedience, you accept us as we are, desiring only what is good – for us and for all. Amen.

343 Take what we are, Lord – with all the dirt that sticks so closely, the ingrained grime that stains our souls – and, by your grace, wash us, and make us clean. Amen.

344 Lord of all, thank you for immersing us in your love, granting peace that lasts not just for a moment, but for ever – rest for our souls. Thank you for your redeeming grace, through which you make all things new, cleansing, transforming and refreshing. Wash us again through your life-giving power, poured out for us and for all. Amen.

345 Sovereign God, we try to hide from you, to evade your searching gaze, but nothing escapes your all-seeing eye. Teach us, though, that we have nothing to fear, for you watch over us not to hurt but to help, not to punish but to pardon. Amen.

346 Merciful God, thank you that, unlike the proverbial leopard, we *can* change our spots; that, through your grace and with your help, we can start again, our inner self transformed, our lives made new. However often it takes, continue to work your miracle of love within us, so that we might become what you would have us be: a little more like you. Amen.

347 Living God, you tell us that humankind is made in your image, created in your likeness, but when we look at who and what we are – our faults and failings – we see little there bearing any resemblance to you. Forgive what is wrong in our lives, and transform it from within, so that, by the miracle of your grace, your will may be done, and something of *you* be seen in us. Amen.

348 Gracious God, thank you that you shut the door on no one, leaving them out in the cold; that, however often we go astray, we have only to call for help, genuinely seeking forgiveness, and you are there, waiting to welcome us home. Amen.

349 Lord Jesus Christ, thank you that your gifts are truly free: your love, mercy, joy and peace – blessings too many to number – offered without strings attached. Thank you for paying the price of these yourself, sharing our flesh, bearing our pain and dying our death, so that we might receive life, now and for all eternity, a prize indeed too special to miss. Amen.

Greatness of God

see also Glory of God, glimpsing; Nature and the environment; Power of God

350 Awesome God, awaken us to your greatness, your majestic power that fills the universe. Teach us to worship and acclaim you as King of kings and Lord of lords. Amen.

351 Sovereign God, we fall down before you in humble worship, for you are sovereign over all, higher than our highest thoughts, greater than we can comprehend or even imagine. To you be honour, glory, acclaim and adoration, now and always. Amen.

352 Loving God, we lift to you our hearts, our minds, our souls, our *selves*, reaching out in joyful praise and grateful worship. Amen.

353 Almighty God, save us from setting anyone up on a pedestal, whoever they may be – from mistaking the trappings of faith for what gives true meaning to life. Remind us that you alone are God, worthy of honour, glory and worship, and may we revere you and none other. Amen.

354 Generous God, your blessings are beyond measure, more than the sand on the seashore, the waves on the ocean, the clouds in the sky, the stars in the heavens. In reverent wonder we give you our praise. Amen.

355 Creator God, save us from becoming too familiar with you, too comfortable and casual in your presence. Remind us of who and what you are, and give us a due sense of awe and reverence. Amen

356 Thank you Lord that, however hard we try, we can never exhaust your greatness, for you are higher than our highest thoughts, beyond anything our mind can reach. Amen.

357 Almighty God, give us a sense of awe in your presence, a glimpse of your greatness and grandeur. Save us from so forgetting who and what you are that we stand before you and fail to marvel. Amen.

358 Mighty and mysterious God, thank you for the capacity of humankind to explore profound mysteries, our ability constantly to push back the boundaries of comprehension. But thank you also for your incomparable greatness – the unfathomable immensity of your love, awesome breadth of your purpose and staggering scale of your power. You are higher than our highest thoughts, above all, before all and beyond all. Receive our praise. Amen.

Growth in grace

see also Commitment; Discipleship, journey of

359 Transforming God, clothe us with what beautifies not the body but the spirit: love, gentleness, compassion, generosity – whatever brings honour to you and promotes your kingdom. Instead of merely looking or feeling the part, may we be truly different, changed from within by your renewing grace. Amen.

360 Loving God, guide us, for time after time we go astray, unthinkingly following the crowd. Help us to copy not the sheep but the shepherd. Amen.

361 Eternal God, give us the maturity of age yet freshness of youth, the wisdom of experience yet innocence of childhood. However many our years of faith, may our love for you and our desire to know you better be as vibrant as the day they were born, the life you have put within us remaining ever old yet ever new. Amen.

362 Sovereign God, we've moved on in much, but have we moved on in *faith*? Have we left former ways behind, or do we *play* at discipleship, treating it as a game instead of being serious about commitment? Have we matured as people, growing up not only as individuals but also in our dealings with others, or do we still lack maturity, being even infantile sometimes in our behaviour? Teach us to be child*like* in attitude but not child*ish*; to display the trust, innocence and enthusiasm of youth, yet also the wisdom, sensitivity and understanding of later years. Amen.

363 Living God, instruct us through your Holy Spirit, for we are slow to learn and struggle to understand. Teach us your way – what it means to love you – so that we may know you better and serve you more faithfully. Grant wisdom, also, so that we may make sense of faith despite all the complexities of this world – the doubts we have and the questions these throw up. Help us to grasp more clearly who and what you are: what you have done, what you mean and who you call us to be. Amen.

364 Creator God, there is little harvest in our lives, and that which there has been is nothing special. But if fruits are missing, may there at least be blossom, some sign of future growth; and though we will always fall short, may something of your beauty be seen in us. Amen.

365 Gracious God, you weigh our lives in the balance, measuring who and what we are. You search us deep within, examining the workings of our minds, our innermost thoughts. Put a new heart and a right spirit within us, and teach us to hunger for food that truly satisfies, nourishing the soul and making us whole. Teach us to love you better, so that when you put us on the scales we will not be found wanting. Amen.

366 Lord Jesus Christ, shine upon us so that our lives may reflect your love, grace, goodness and mercy. Open our hearts to the light of your presence, so that who and what we are may speak of you and your glory. Amen.

367 Almighty God, teach us more of *you* and instruct us in your ways. Open our hearts and minds to your guidance, and give us a receptive spirit, so that we may learn to know you better, grasping more of your will and growing in faith and understanding. Remind us that, however much we have fathomed of your purpose or experienced of your love, there is more still to discover, more than we can ever hope to comprehend. Amen.

368 Loving God, thank you for preparing the ground in our lives – not only sowing the seed, but also doing the spadework beforehand in order for your love to take root and grow within us. Continue what you have begun, cultivating your word of life in our hearts, so that, in the fullness of time, we may bear a harvest pleasing to you. Amen.

369 Lord Jesus Christ, teach us to follow where you lead, to walk in your footsteps, thinking as *you* would think, speaking as you would speak and doing as you would do. Help us to be more like you. Amen.

370 Almighty God, we're good at feeding our body, if careless sometimes what we eat, but when it comes to our soul it's a sorrier tale. Turning our back on food that satisfies – living bread, true sustenance – we cram ourselves instead with junk food, a diet that, instead of nourishing, undermines health, leaving us spiritually flabby, inwardly weak. Forgive us, and teach us to feast at your table instead of snacking on empty morsels. Amen.

371 Living God, teach us that we must be vigilant if the tender shoots of faith are not to be overwhelmed. Faults and weaknesses, though conquered for a time, are rarely eliminated – each awaiting their moment, ready to burst into life when our backs are turned and to take over again. Save us, then, from complacency, and keep us alert to whatever may undermine the life you have sown within us, so that it may not simply grow but, above all, flourish. Amen.

372 Are you there, Lord? Are you watching, listening, speaking your word? We look, but do not see, hope, but wait in vain, yet still we sense your presence. Give us a heart and mind to know you better. Amen.

373 Gracious God, draw us closer to you and to those around us, overcoming whatever keeps us apart and uniting us in love. Amen.

374 Renewing God, fashion us by the touch of your hand, and finish your new creation. Take who we are, and from the deadwood of our lives craft something beautiful for you. Amen.

375 Loving God, for all our talk of closeness, the relationship between us is more like a tug of war than a shared embrace, a broken marriage than a match made in heaven, for, despite our best intentions, we constantly pull away from you, resisting your will and attempting to impose ours in its place. Teach us that, however hard we strive against you, you will never let go, and so may we learn to work *with* rather than *against* you. Amen.

376 Merciful God, forgive us, for we've become complacent, assuming we've grasped all we need to know, no longer novices in discipleship but graduates, our education complete. Teach us that, for all our years of faith, there is more still to be learnt, much that we've barely begun to explore. Instruct us, then, in your ways, and lead us to ever-deeper understanding. Amen.

377 Give us wings like eagles, Lord, so that our imagination may take flight, our horizons reach ever higher, and our spirits soar to you. Lift us above the things of this earth so that we may catch a glimpse of your kingdom above, life here and now being shaped by a vision of life to come. Amen.

378 Mighty God, grant us strength of faith, character, wisdom and purpose, coupled with a gentleness of spirit; an inner steel matched by tenderness and humility in our dealings with others. Though we are weak, may we be strong in you. Amen.

379 Help us, Lord, for we're torn two ways, your love tugging at our hearts but temptation pulling us away. Deepen our faith and increase our commitment, so that our will may be one with yours. Amen.

380 Eternal God, however old we may be, keep us young in faith – childlike in trust and eager to grow. Amen.

381 Loving God, instead of settling for a superficial faith, may we dig deeper, looking always to discover new delights, fresh food for our souls. Amen.

382 Forgive us, Lord, for we've leant on you too heavily, treating you as some kind of prop. Help us to stand on our own two feet, and to step out in faith. Amen.

383 Teach us more of your way, Lord, more of your truth, for however much we've understood, there's far more still to learn. Amen.

384 Creator God, just as we need to feed and water the plants in our garden if they're to flourish as they should, teach us also to nurture our faith through time with you, so that it too may blossom and bloom. Amen.

385 Give us enquiring minds, Lord: an innate curiosity to learn about you and to know you better. We've glimpsed a little: help us to see more. Amen.

386 Lord Jesus Christ, help us to imitate your example – to follow you faithfully, seeking in all we think, say and do to become more like you. Amen.

387 Lord of all, keep us young at heart, innocent, trusting and eager to learn. Though we grow old in body may we stay youthful in spirit and childlike in faith. Amen.

388 Living God, no one will ever confuse the two of us, but help us at least to resemble you; not in outward appearance, but in the people we are, the things we think and feel, say and do. Poor though the likeness will always be, may something in our lives speak of you, reminding others of the love and care you have for all. Amen.

389 Loving God, we let you down, for though we talk of bearing fruit the reality is different, any harvest we produce being a mere apology. Nurture and nourish our faith, so that it may truly grow. Amen.

390 Gracious God, you do not expect us to be just like you, and you do not want all your people to be clones, each thinking and acting the same, but you *do* want something of Christ to show in the lives of those who follow you. Work within us, so that, despite all that mars the picture, at least a little of his love, joy and goodness may shine through. Amen.

391 Loving God, prune the deadwood and all redundant growth from our lives. Though the process may be painful and the measures severe, trim back whatever undermines true health and wholeness, so that we may reach greater maturity in faith and become more fully the people you want us to be. Amen.

392 Mighty and mysterious God, remind us that whatever we have glimpsed of your goodness, much yet remains hidden, still to be discovered. Teach us to keep on exploring, so that we may learn more of you each day. Amen.

393 Creator God, save us from dwelling on ourselves – our interests, our ideas, our image. Make our lives a mirror, reflecting you and you alone. Amen.

394 Lord Jesus Christ, take what we are and shape what we shall be. Little by little, help us to become more like you. Amen.

395 Teach us, Lord, to feed not only our body but also our soul, to pay as much attention to spiritual sustenance as to physical, so that, properly nourished each day, we may grow healthy and strong in faith. Amen.

396 Creator God, remind us that, just as we need to care for our gardens if everything is to flourish there as it should, so also we must nurture our faith if that too is to blossom and bloom. Teach us, then, to set aside time to pray and reflect, to study your word, seek your guidance and understand your will. Teach us, above all, to make time for you, so that the seed you have sown in our hearts may grow to fruition. Amen.

397 Living God, too often we're preoccupied with self and how others see us. Help us instead to think first of you, and to reflect something of your love and goodness in who and what we are. Amen.

398 Gracious God, we want to grow in faith, to mature and flourish in discipleship, so that our lives bear fruit for you, but however hard we try, we cannot do it alone. Nurture the seed you have sown within us and bring it to fulfilment. Amen.

399 Mighty and mysterious God, thank you that whatever we know of you, there is more still to learn; that however much we've understood we're still just beginners in faith. Amen.

400 All-seeing God, teach us to listen not just to those who praise us but to those who see our faults; to remember that an honest critic can be our truest friend, pointing not simply to what we *like* to hear but what we *need* to hear if we would truly grow. Amen.

401 Lord Jesus Christ, what do people see in us beneath the mask of piety and veneer of commitment? What picture do we give them? What image of you do we convey? Forgive us, for too often it's a caricature, a false and flawed reflection, giving altogether the wrong impression. Move in us, and help us to be more like you. Amen.

402 You call us, Lord, to clothe ourselves with gentleness, love, patience, humility, kindness and self-control. Help us not just to toy with such garments, trying them on for a moment only to discard them afterwards, but to wear them each day – inner clothes that truly make a difference to who we are. Amen.

403 Loving God, you offer food for our souls, but too often we expect to be spoon-fed, everything served up for us on a plate. Forgive us and help us to understand that, if we want to grow, as well as hungering after righteousness, we must learn to feed ourselves. Through prayer, worship, and the study of your word, help us each day to taste of your love and know more of your goodness. Amen.

Guidance

see also Discipleship, journey of

404 Almighty God, despite the maze of options that daily confronts us, we feel confident of taking the right path and negotiating our way safely through the labyrinth. Yet plans have a habit of going astray, few things working out as we would like, so that, once more, we end up lost and confused, uncertain where to turn next. In all the complexities each day brings, the moral and ethical dilemmas, the confusing choices and life-shaping decisions, grant us your guidance and see us safely through. Amen.

405 Loving God, ferry us through the straits of life, for we cannot get through alone. In calm or tempest, sunshine or rain, carry us safely over the waters until we reach the shore and set foot in your kingdom. Amen.

406 Teach us, Lord, that two heads are better than one, able, when put together, to come up with answers that escape us on our own. Help us, then, to work with others, and, above all, with you. Amen.

407 Lord Jesus Christ, thank you for having gone ahead of us, walking this earth, sharing our humanity, experiencing testing, temptation, pain and sorrow, even to the very darkness of death. Teach us to follow where you lead, to walk in your footsteps, thinking as *you* would think, speaking as you would speak and doing as you would do. Guide us always, and lead us safely to our journey's end. Amen.

408 Living God, help us, for despite all the effort we put into life and faith we seem sometimes to be going round and round in circles, getting nowhere. Grant your guidance and lead us forward. Amen.

409 Mighty and mysterious God, give us wisdom to know you, intelligence to understand you better, perception to grasp your will, and discernment to follow you faithfully. Protect, provide, instruct, direct, so that, even in life's darkest moments, we may follow your way and respond to your guidance. Amen.

410 Eternal God, we can try to plan ahead, predict the future, and yes, at times, make a decent fist of it, but in things that really matter, life-shaping events and issues, we can rarely be confident, still less sure. Teach us that, though we may map our intended path, it is you who directs our steps, and you alone who holds the future in your hands. Amen.

411 Lord Jesus Christ, you try to guide us, to shepherd us in the right direction, but time and again we simply ignore you. Help us to recognise your presence, and to respond. Amen.

412 Loving God, we don't always welcome your discipline or respect your authority, attempting instead to go our own way, do our own thing. Keep watch and show us where we go astray. Correct us, punish where necessary, and help us to follow the rules you have set – if not for your sake, then for ours. Amen.

413 Merciful God, we feel sometimes that life is a dead end, a road to nowhere. We stride out confidently, believing we know the best way forward, only to be pulled up short, stopped in our tracks by some disappointment, problem or tragedy, and we're left asking, 'What now?' 'Why are we here?' 'Where next?' Speak to us when life seems bereft of meaning and purpose. Direct our steps, give light to our path and lead us in your eternal way. Amen.

414 Sovereign God, when it comes to knowing you, to growing in faith, we need help to get the picture, for there are gaps in our knowledge, details we find hard to grasp, not least in the study of your word. Teach us to appreciate those who offer guidance – preachers, teachers, scholars, writers – all whose insights lead to deeper perception and a fuller experience of your love, and, in humility, may we listen and learn. Amen.

415 Gracious God, you set boundaries for us, not to restrict or confine but to give definition to who and what we are – your love being the space in which we live, your guidance giving parameters to our lives and your mercy placing us back within them when we step over the line. For the meaning and direction we find in you, receive our praise. Amen.

416 Loving God, show us the way we should go, for so often we lose our bearings, wilfully taking the wrong road or wandering aimlessly through life. When we mistake the path or stray from it, remind us that you are the way that leads to life, and may that knowledge guide our footsteps. Amen.

417 Teach us, Lord; instruct, control and direct; so that *your* will may be our will, and our way, your way. Amen.

418 Living God, thank you for the guidance you offer each day, not setting out detailed instructions for every aspect of life, still less dictating the course we should take, but prompting through your word and pointing the way forward. Teach us to travel in faith until the journey is done, your love offering a light to our path, a compass through the changing scenes of life. Amen.

419 Lord Jesus Christ, we thought we were making progress, but we were wrong – we're going round in circles, getting nowhere. Show us the way to life. Amen.

420 When we go astray and stumble into danger, Lord, guide our footsteps and see us safely through. Amen.

421 Saviour Christ, you try to guide us, to shepherd us in the right direction, but so often we go astray or resist your will, foolish, obstinate, rebellious. In your mercy, deal gently with our faults and restore us to your side. Show us the way you would have us take and help us to walk it faithfully. Amen.

Hope and trust

see also Faithfulness of God; New beginnings

422 Living God, help us to dream dreams, not as a form of escapism but in order to glimpse your purpose and understand more of your transforming love; to catch sight of all you are able to do and all we can become; to recognise that there is more to life than our senses can grasp – things too wonderful for us as yet to fathom. Give us a vision of the future and confidence that you will turn dreams into reality. Amen.

423 Eternal God, thank you that we can look forward with expectation, confident that the future is in your hands – that, as you have blessed us, so you will bless us again, each day bringing new beginnings. Amen.

424 Lord of all, teach us that you are a God who repeatedly turns the tables, the way of Christ, if taken seriously, challenging the assumptions of this world and upsetting the status quo. Teach us that, though it may not sometimes seem like it, you will finally correct injustice, overcome evil and undo wrongs, in your kingdom the first being last and the last first. Help us, then, to trust in your purpose and to walk humbly with you. Amen.

425 Everlasting God, so much in life proves impossible to hold on to. We think it's ours, safely secured, only for it to slip away – here one minute and gone the next. Teach us to celebrate the joys of this world but to root our happiness in what lies beyond it – in your love that never ends and that nothing can take away. Amen.

426 Thank you, Lord, that we can rest easy, secure in your love, knowing that whatever we face, in life or in death, you will be with us, now and always. Amen.

427 Gracious God, in the rollercoaster of life, with all its thrills and spills, teach us to take the ups with the downs, recognising that sorrow is sometimes the price of joy, and pain the corollary of pleasure. However deep the troughs or sudden the fall, help us to keep faith, confident you hold fresh heights in store, until we ascend into the fullness of your kingdom for evermore. Amen.

428 Eternal God, you promise us a home not made with human hands but kept in heaven; a house with many rooms, where we will dwell in the light of your love for evermore. We're not sure of the details – where or when it will be, or what form life will take there – but that's not important, for you tell us all we need to know. In that assurance we put our trust. Amen.

429 Loving Lord, keep alive in us the hopefulness of youth, that same sense of joy in simple things and expectation for the future. Though life dishes out knocks and disappointments, help us to carry on believing in what you hold in store – wonderful beyond words. Amen.

430 God of past, present and future, remind us that in this world we're merely passing through; that, for all its beauty and wonder – the countless joys it has to offer – it's not our final destination but a staging post along the way. Teach us, then, to celebrate everything it has to offer, yet not to be bound by it, to savour its many riches, but never to confuse them with blessings still to come. Amen.

431 Gracious God, you have granted us a glimpse of your kingdom through the life of Christ and the witness of Scripture. Not a complete portrait, still less every detail, but enough to give an impression of its splendour, a flavour of the joy, refreshment and tranquillity it holds in store. May that snapshot capture our imagination and sustain our faith, this and every day. Amen.

432 Lord of heaven and earth, so much in life seems special, hard to resist, and we try to pack as much in as possible, afraid of missing out. Yet however beguiling present joys may be, save us from confusing pleasure now with treasure to come, the attractions of this world with the riches of your kingdom. Remind us that each is but a foretaste of delights to come, too many to number, too wonderful to contemplate. Amen.

433 Help us to live in this world, Lord, celebrating all it has to offer, yet still to look to you, keeping in sight things above. Amen.

434 Loving God, when we're nervous, fearful about the future and our ability to meet it, teach us to believe in ourselves – to have the same faith in us as you have. Amen.

435 Almighty God, teach us that this world is not our home; that, for all the blessings it offers, we are simply passing through. Help us to celebrate the joys of life, but never to forget that they are fleeting, here today and gone tomorrow. Remind us that only your word endures for ever – your love, your truth, your kingdom – and so may we walk the pilgrim way, journeying ultimately to your eternal city where we shall dwell with you for evermore. Amen.

436 Redeemer God, thank you for offering so much more than vague optimism – not just wishful thinking, hoping against hope, but true promise for the future, a confidence in your purpose that will not disappoint. Thank you that though life's dreams may come to nothing, though heaven and earth should pass away, your love endures for ever, and the joys of your kingdom will never disappoint. Amen.

437 Sovereign God, we try to protect ourselves against the vagaries life, for there's no telling what tomorrow might bring, but, of course, we can't, for however much we try to safeguard earthly possessions, they can be plucked from us so swiftly, this mortal span being like a passing shadow and our hold on this world tenuous at best. Yes, we must look after our loved ones, ensuring their security as far as we can, but remind us of what really counts, of the true and lasting treasures found in you alone, and teach us to prize those above all else, knowing that you are able to keep them safe not just now but for all eternity. Amen.

438 Whatever our stage of life, Lord, help us to greet it thankfully, knowing that as you have blessed us so you will bless us again – each moment given by you, and with the best yet to come. Amen.

439 Loving God, when life brings bad news, disappointment, trouble or tragedy, bring comfort, strength, hope and healing – faith that joy will come again. Amen.

440 Gracious God, remind us that, in this life, there can be no sun without shadow or laughter without tears, and that sometimes the darkness seems deeper the more the light shines. Teach us, then, however dark the shade, to keep faith, trusting that, despite appearances, you are there. Amen.

441 Lord of heaven and earth, you alone are eternal, the same yesterday, today and tomorrow. You alone are before and beyond all, the beginning and end of everything that is, has been and shall be. Yet you invite us – seemingly here today and gone tomorrow, like flowers fleetingly in bloom – to share in eternity, one with you for evermore. For the breadth of your purpose and wonder of your grace, thank you. Amen.

442 Eternal God, thank you for offering us not just wishful thinking, hope against hope, but true promise for the future, a confidence in your purpose that will not disappoint. Amen.

443 Lord Jesus Christ, just as, when we swim, we trust ourselves to the water, confident it will support us if we keep faith, help us to trust you in turn, assured that you will do the same. Amen.

444 Everlasting God, teach us that though we can shape the present and influence the future, we can control neither. Help us to recognise what's beyond us, and to leave such things in your hands, where they belong. Amen.

445 Faithful God, thank you that we can face each day with confidence, knowing that whatever swings and roundabouts we may face, whatever twists and turns, highs and lows, you will be with us through them all. Amen.

Intercession

see also Relationships

For those addicted to alcohol or drugs

446 Living God, to all who seek pleasure through intoxication, blotting out perception to fill the void within, grant genuine fulfilment. Pour into their hearts the sparkling wine of your love that they may find true life, their cup spilling over, full to overflowing. Amen.

447 Lord Jesus Christ, reach out to all who, seeking freedom and fulfilment, abuse their bodies to escape them; all who, in their search for happiness, are vulnerable to unscrupulous predators. Help them to get a buzz out of life not through artificial means, chemically induced elation, but through experiencing the thrill of your presence, and tasting the inner ecstasy that you alone can bring. Amen.

For the ageing

448 Eternal God, hear our prayer for those in their twilight years, the sun beginning to set though yet not gone down. Though the energy of youth is long past and aspirations of middle years seem distant, may this time of life bring joys of its own: an inner tranquillity and contentment in light of all that has gone before, coupled with confident trust in what is yet to come – the new dawn that, by your grace, will surely follow the night. Amen.

449 Gracious God, when strength fails and faculties diminish, advancing years taking their toll, remind us that you bring new beginnings, life that will never fade. Amen.

For those broken by life

450 Loving God, reach out to those who have lost the will to live, all who are broken in body, mind or spirit, seeing no hope, no future, no reason to continue. Lift their despair, and may they find in you a life that satisfies, now and always. Amen.

451 Saviour Christ, so many in life are worn to breaking point, ground down by sickness, hurt, worry and fear, by the ravages of time, and uncertain how much longer they can cope. Reach out to strengthen and restore, from the tangled threads of their lives weaving cords that will not be broken. Amen.

452 Lord Jesus Christ, as you touched the untouchables throughout your ministry, so you reach out still, seeing not the affliction but the person underneath. Forgive the feebleness of our love, and teach us to do the same. Amen.

453 Loving God, when hearts are broken, lives wrecked by sickness, fear, hurt and sorrow, people can break down completely, the business of repair a long and uncertain business. Reach out to all who feel they cannot carry on, and give them strength not just to resume their journey but to embark on it with confidence renewed and anticipation restored, able to see it safely through until they reach the end. Amen.

454 Lord Jesus Christ, when love brings hurt, the pain of rejection, betrayal or loss, may *your* love bring comfort, and help to heal the wounds. Amen.

455 Renewing God, so many find their lives shattered – broken by the loss of a loved one, accident or injury, the onset of disease or the breakdown of relationships – and though sometimes they can be restored and the pieces put back together, sometimes they can't, in this life, at least, the damage being too great to mend. Reach out into fragmented hearts, bringing healing and hope, until that day when your kingdom comes, and all is made whole. Amen.

For our broken world

456 Creator God, heal our broken world, and put an end to its madness, so that, whatever divides, and whatever our colour, creed or culture, we may see beyond cause or grievance to the common humanity that unites us all. Amen.

457 Loving God, our world lies broken, fractured by prejudice, splintered by hate, scarred by fear, and for all our efforts we cannot make it whole. Pick up the pieces and bind them together, bringing healing where there is hurt and unity where there is division. Hear our prayer and honour our hopes. Amen.

458 Overcome what keeps us apart, Lord. Turn fear to trust, hate to love and war to peace. Amen.

459 Lord Jesus Christ, reach out to our broken world – scarred by hatred, fractured by division, ravaged by war – and, in your mercy, grant us peace. Amen.

460 Merciful God, thank you for the knowledge that you are always there, ready to carry us when we cannot continue, to tend our wounds when we lie bruised and broken, to provide healing and renewal in body, mind and spirit. Teach us to minister to life's casualties in turn, reaching out with supportive hands and caring touch, in your name. Amen.

461 Lord of all, there is so much evil in our world yet so much good, so much ugliness yet so much beauty. Nurture whatever enriches and builds up, and overcome that which demeans and degrades. Amen.

462 Loving God, we see news pictures day after day of hunger, squalor, violence and suffering beamed into our living rooms from across the world, and our hearts go out to those enduring such misery. But we are able to turn away, dismissing such things from our minds. Only there's no such option for them: this is the daily reality of their lives. Remind us that they are real people, each one our neighbour, and instead of pushing them aside, as if they are part of another world, teach us, whenever and wherever we can, to respond in love. Amen.

463 Holy God, our world is stained, engulfed by a black tide of injustice, intolerance, fear and hatred that desecrates and destroys countless lives and, for all our so-called advances, we're no nearer containing it than we've ever been. Come to our aid, and cleanse us of all that denies and divides – that precludes joy and crushes hope. Transform what we can never change ourselves, and make all things new. Amen.

464 Lord of all, overcome the barriers that keep us apart, dividing person from person and race from race – East and West, black and white, male and female, rich and poor. Whatever our colour, culture or creed, draw us together and heal our wounds – so that we may live and work together as one people, one world. Amen.

465 Lord of the nations, when we consider the scale of human need, the enormous suffering, injustice and deprivation faced by so many, we feel despondent, overwhelmed, for we seem powerless to change anything, to do anything meaningful to help. The world is so big, and we are so small, insignificant in terms of the forces that shape and control it. Help us, nonetheless, in our living and loving, our speaking and doing, to work for change, in partnership with you and others. Remind us that what *we* can't do, *you* can. Amen.

For carers

466 Living God, hear our prayer for carers, those who devote so much of their lives to looking after loved ones – parents, partners, children, friends – often at immense personal cost. Strengthen them, that may find the reserves to continue. Minister to them, so that they may minister in turn. In all they do, may they be sustained by the knowledge that they too are loved, they too are cared for – by you. Amen.

For the homeless

467 Reach out, Lord, to those who walk the streets – young people who've run away from home, vagrants sleeping rough, the destitute and dispossessed. Remind them that though they may not have a roof over their head, they have a place in your heart, each of them being important to you. Bless the work of churches, charities, hostels and agencies – all who strive to provide food and shelter, and who offer the prospect of new beginnings, opportunities for the future. Teach us where and how we can best respond to others, and so also to you. Amen.

For the lonely

468 Saviour Christ, reach out to the lonely, those who look out in vain for a knock at the door, a friendly face, a moment of company. However isolated they may be, teach them that you are by their side. Amen.

For peace and harmony

see also Relationships; Remembrance Day

469 Lord Jesus Christ, despised and rejected during your ministry, reach out to the marginalised – those pushed to the edge of society, their identity denied, rights ignored and dignity destroyed. Overcome the barriers of fear, suspicion and prejudice that divide us, estranging person from person, community from community, and, whatever our differences, help us to recognise the true worth of all – to see beyond what keeps us apart to the common humanity that binds us together. Amen.

470 Healing God, bring closer the day when our divisions will be overcome, our differences put aside, and our fear and mistrust ended – a time when we will live in peace together, and you will be all in all. Amen.

471 Lord of all, grant not just peace but reconciliation in our world, an end to all that divides and destroys, so that those previously estranged may come together, shoulder to shoulder, heart to heart. Amen.

472 Lord Jesus Christ, in a world of conflict where so many are at loggerheads, tussling for power and prestige, bring an end to division. Put an end to our posturing, our endless conflict and confrontation, and show us the way to peace. Amen.

473 Gracious God, in a divided world, where chasms of fear, hatred, envy and injustice come between so many, help us to build bridges – to do what we can, where we can, to construct links, create dialogue and promote partnership, bringing together those previously kept apart. Where barriers estrange and rifts alienate, help us to be peacemakers. Amen.

474 Renewing God, grant not just superficial peace in our world, but reconciliation, an end to whatever divides and destroys – all that fosters hatred, intolerance and injustice leading to misery for so many. Break down religious, ethnic and social barriers, so that those previously estranged may come together, moving beyond their differences to a genuine meeting of minds, and harmony among all. Amen.

475 Loving God, reach out to our broken world – scarred by suspicion, fractured by hatred, ravaged by cruelty, violence and war – and, in your mercy, heal our wounds, overcome our divisions, and grant us real and lasting peace. Amen.

For the poor and hungry

see also Grace before meals

476 Mighty God, in a world where the powerful prosper and the weak are exploited, teach us to think generously, deal gently and love all. Amen.

477 Lord of all, we think of the millions in this world for whom water is a luxury. We think of dehydrated children, dying of thirst, of communities whose supplies are polluted and diseased, of lands parched, pasture turned to dust. And we're ashamed, for, like so many, we're swift to bemoan our lot and slow to count our blessings. Teach us to understand how lucky we are and to think, for a change, of others instead of ourselves. Amen.

478 Forgive us, Lord, for in a world of need, of hunger, injustice and oppression, we turn our back on others, concerned solely with our own welfare. Remind us that in ignoring them, we ignore you too. Amen.

479 Loving God, we know that if evils are to be tackled it needs the will of politicians, governments and leaders, and we pray that they'll do their bit. We know it needs fairer trade and relief of debt coupled with generous, genuine aid, and we pray these will be achieved. But save us from using all this to pass the buck, as though the ills of this world are not also down to us. As well as *calling* for change, help us to change in turn, ready to play our part before we ask others to play *theirs*. Amen.

480 Lord of the nations, we speak of making poverty history, and we've done that, but not in the way intended. We've made it part of our world, an accepted norm, a fact of life . . . and death . . . for countless millions, and though it's not all our doing, much of it being down to forces beyond our control, we're all still complicit in the crime, none of us able to absolve ourselves fully of responsibility. Forgive the evil of our world, and our share within it, and give us all a common resolve to tackle poverty and *truly* consign it to history. Amen.

481 Merciful God, we've made progress, but not much, each of us still being part of a wasteful culture, a society built on disposability that consumes resources with little thought of tomorrow and still less for others. Give us a greater sense of responsibility to future generations and to you; an appreciation of the countless blessings we have received and the duty we have to use them wisely, so that others may enjoy them in turn. Amen.

482 Lord of all, in a world where so many cannot fight their corner; where the rich prosper and the poor are crushed, the strong thrive and the weak go to the wall; where naked self-interest leads to friendships being broken, people estranged, societies divided and nations driven to conflict; teach us your way of love and humility, of putting the interests of others before our own. If we would serve *you*, teach us to serve *all*. Amen.

483 Loving God, when we fill our trolley, when we queue at the checkout, when we unpack and restock our cupboards at home, help us to remember those whose provisions for a day, a week, even a month, would fit into one shopping bag several times over. Remind us that what we see as a snack is a luxury for others, that our meal for one could feed a family of many. Help us not just to *remember* those with so much less, but to share with them from our plenty. Amen.

For scientists and researchers

484 Creator God, the powers of modern science scare but excite us, for they have potential for both good and evil, being able to enrich life or undermine it, to transform yet destroy. Give wisdom to all scientists and researchers, and to those who set laws regulating their activities, so that the skills you have given may be used responsibly and for the good of all. Amen.

For those searching for meaning

485 Mighty and mysterious God, for many life feels like an incomplete jigsaw – frustrating, disappointing, infuriating. For all their striving, they feel unfulfilled, as if a component is missing, and though they cannot quite place what it is, they search hungrily for that special something, that elusive final piece to complete the picture. Draw near to them, so that in you they may find what they seek: the One who satisfies our inner yearning, and gives meaning to all. Amen.

For the sick and those who tend them

486 To all under the weather, Lord – all who are sick or suffering – give strength, help, love and healing. Amen.

487 Loving God, reach out to the incapacitated – those injured through accident, wounded in war, maimed through illness, or deformed at birth. Equip them to face the challenges life brings, and to see themselves, however disfigured they may be, as whole people, precious in your sight. Amen.

488 Eternal God, to all wrestling with terminal illness, give the assurance that you will always value them for who they are; and help their families, friends and colleagues, as they struggle to come to terms with their feelings, to do the same, seeing not the illness but the individual underneath. Whatever else may be lost, may that continue, to the end and beyond. Amen.

489 Lord Jesus Christ, hear our prayer for the sick – all who are in pain, waiting for or recovering from surgery, undergoing treatment or coming to terms with terminal illness. Give help and strength to any whose health is failing, and to all who tend them. Amen.

490 Compassionate God, forgive us, for we forget those who live in constant pain, longing for release yet finding no end to their suffering, each day blighted by its stranglehold. Give them strength not just to get through but also to find joy and fulfilment in life, and grant the assurance that, just as you shared our sufferings in Christ, so, through him, we will all finally enter a brighter kingdom in which pain and sorrow will be at an end. Amen.

491 Loving God, for those troubled about their health, and those with the responsibility of ministering to them, grant your help, guidance and love. Amen.

492 Lord Jesus Christ, who shed your blood for all, thank you for those who donate theirs to others in turn, from so simple an offering coming so special a gift to so great a multitude. Inspire us, if we are able, to do the same. Amen.

493 God of grace and mercy, reach out to all in hospital: the sick and frail; those waiting for an operation, fearful about the procedure or the future; those recovering from major surgery, wrestling with chronic disease or struggling with pain; those coming to terms with terminal illness. Work through nurses, doctors, surgeons and support staff, through counsellors, ministers, friends and family, and, through your Holy Spirit, to bring comfort, strength, relief and healing. Through your love and that of others, grant to all facing ill health the knowledge that they are not alone. Amen.

494 Healing God, hear our prayer for the sick – all who are in pain, waiting for or recovering from surgery, undergoing long-term treatment, battling against disease, anxious about the future. Support them through family and friends, through the skill and dedication of medical staff, and, above all, through the knowledge of your love. Minister your healing touch, and grant them the peace and strength they need to find wholeness in you. Amen.

495 Lord Jesus Christ, hear our prayer for those in our hospitals: for patients and their loved ones, but, above all, for those who staff them – those with the courage to face, day after day, the sheer intensity of it all, striving with such dedication to nurture wholeness in body, mind and spirit. Thank you for their skill and compassion; the renewal they bring, life they make possible, understanding they show and comfort they extend. Thank you for their willingness to care for others. Amen.

For those who feel trapped

496 Redeemer God, reach out to those who feel trapped, imprisoned by circumstances, held captive by past mistakes, present worries or future prospects. Give to them and to all the liberty that you alone can give, your truth that sets us free. Amen.

497 Living God, we feel trapped sometimes, imprisoned in our own small world. Reach out to all who feel separated from others and from you; come and set them free. Amen.

For those who mourn

498 Eternal God, in the ugliness of death speak of life born again, and in the apparent finality of the grave point to new beginnings. To all who mourn give the assurance that the close of one chapter is the opening of another, this world being the gateway to your eternal kingdom. Amen.

499 Gracious God, we need to grieve when we lose loved ones, for the sorrow is real, the pain hard to bear; but we also need to rejoice, for with you death is not the end but a new beginning. The shell is empty but has nurtured life; the casket is bare but its treasure is safe in your hands; the person we knew we will know again, for they are truly at home, secure in your everlasting arms, alive with all your people, for evermore. May that truth comfort and strengthen those who mourn, giving them the assurance that nothing finally can separate us from your love in Christ. Amen.

500 Everlasting God, remind us that even in the darkest days of life and the bleak chill of death, you are there, bringing new beginnings. For your life-giving power, beyond containment, receive our praise. Amen.

501 Caring God, thank you for the assurance that in times of sorrow you will be there to comfort – ready to mend our broken hearts and bring us joy once more. Amen.

502 Lord Jesus Christ, thank you for your promise of comfort. Reach out to all who mourn, and turn their sorrow to joy, their tears to laughter and their despair to hope. Amen.

503 God of all comfort, when we despair, life bringing hurt and sorrow, give us strength to continue, until light dawns, hope returns and tears are wiped away. Amen.

Joy and celebration

504 Loving God, despite the tragedies of this world, the trials we personally may face, help us still to see the funny side of life, and to celebrate your gift of laughter. For everything that puts a smile on our faces and joy in our hearts, thank you. Amen.

505 Forgive us, Lord, for so often we greet the morning with a groan and a grimace. Teach us instead to awake with a song in our hearts, celebrating the new dawn you make possible each day. Amen.

506 Lord of all, keep us ever-enthused, ever-excited, by the message of your love – what you have done and continue to do through Christ our Lord. Amen.

507 Eternal God, we carry a host of memories in our hearts – so much we have done, so many we have known, innumerable people, places, sights and sounds that have enriched and enthralled, fashioning the people we are today. For all we have so richly received, thank you. Amen.

508 Lord Jesus Christ, forgive us for taking for granted the little things of life and the health that allows us to experience them. Teach us to celebrate even the simplest of moments, however mundane they may seem. Amen.

509 Gracious God, we have cause to celebrate, for you have blessed us so richly, showering us each day with good things, yet we so rarely appreciate it, let alone show it. We brood instead of rejoice, complain instead of give thanks, our hearts being heavy rather than dancing within us for joy. Forgive us, and teach us to count our blessings and exult in your love. Amen.

510 Living God, help us to spread a little happiness, contagious joy bubbling up within us. Teach us to live with a smile in our hearts and laughter on our lips, each day celebrating your love in a way that invites others to share it in turn. Amen.

511 Loving God, we would sing a new song to you, making music in our hearts in grateful praise and worship. We would make a joyful noise, not to draw attention to ourselves but simply to celebrate your love and to share it with others. Amen.

512 Merciful God, save us from self-pity, from brooding on our troubles and magnifying our woes. If we have cause to feel sorry for ourselves, teach us that we have far more to celebrate and for which to give thanks. Amen.

513 Living God, teach us that true happiness is not a lottery but a gift; not dependent on wealth or possessions but freely available to all; not rooted on earth but kept in heaven, to be tasted now and savoured for all eternity. Teach us to celebrate each day as it comes, rejoicing in all you have lavished upon us and anticipating the treasures yet held in store. Amen.

514 Eternal God, teach us, though our destination lies beyond this world, to celebrate the journey of life, recognising the innumerable ways it can fill us with joy, touch us with wonder and move us to gratitude. Save us from being so full of heaven that we lose sight of earth, from dwelling so much on joys to come that we close our eyes to blessings now. You offer life in all its fullness. Teach us to live it now. Amen.

515 Lord of new beginnings, teach us to greet each day with gratitude, awakening with a sense of joy and expectation at the possibilities of life. Whatever fears we may have or problems we may be facing, help us to welcome the new morning as your gift and to live every moment as fully as we are able. Amen.

516 Loving God, teach us to greet life with a smile, seeing the best rather than the worst, the good instead of the bad. Help us to spread a little happiness through the joy you have poured into our hearts. Amen.

517 Almighty God, thank you for continuing to amaze us, time and again producing yet more blessings out of the hat. Thank you for bringing fresh surprises day after day, greater than we can ask or imagine. Amen.

518 Generous God, thank you, for, by your grace and goodness, you have put music in our souls and a song in our hearts – a melody of praise and thanksgiving at so much that transports us with wonder and thrills us deep within. Keep that joy as fresh in us tomorrow as it is today. Amen.

519 Loving God, thank you that when we smile, the world smiles too; that a cheerful heart brings blessing, not just to us but to others as well. Teach us to celebrate that priceless gift, costing nothing yet yielding so much; to exult in the joy of knowing you and to pass it on in turn. Amen.

520 Thank you, Lord, that with you not just *some* days are special, but *all* of them. You have given us new life, new beginnings, cause indeed to celebrate. Amen.

521 Compassionate God, though much in life is touched by pathos, teach us to keep a sense of humour, able to laugh, even through tears, and smile, even in sorrow. And though much is serious, demanding a measured response and sober judgement, help us to retain a sense of fun, aware that laughter is your gift, as valuable and special as any. Amen.

522 We want to jump for joy, Lord, for you have blessed us with love, filled us with peace and enriched us with hope. For your great goodness and countless gifts, thank you. Amen.

523 Living God, we want to make music for you, to live our lives as an exuberant melody of praise offered in gratitude for all you've done and everything you mean to us. It may sometimes be out of tune, more of a joyful noise than a work of art, but receive it, we pray, together with what we are and all we long to be, for it comes from the heart, with love. Amen.

524 God of grace and mercy, you have given cause to rejoice; forgiveness, new life and blessings beyond measure. Help us to appreciate your goodness and truly to celebrate. Amen.

525 Lord God, you have put a new song into our mouths, a song of joy and thanksgiving, awe and celebration. We will make music to you in our hearts – a melody of praise and worship. Amen.

Judging others

see also Relationships; Worth of all

526 Lord of all, forgive us for the way we pigeonhole people, unconsciously absorbing the prejudices of society even as we resist them, shaped by fears and preconceptions we're not even aware of, hiding behind generalisations that say more about us than others. Open our eyes to see people as they are, rather than as we construe them to be. Amen.

527 Merciful God, forgive us, for we assume that we know others, understand where they're coming from, when in reality we have little idea. Help us truly to get alongside people, putting ourselves as far as we can into their shoes. Before we presume to advise, interfere, judge or condemn, teach us to look at things not from our point of view but from theirs, and to deal as generously with them as you have dealt with us. Amen.

528 Welcoming God, in a host of ways we can be prickly sometimes, easily needled, often defensive and all too swift to turn *in* on ourselves and *against* others. Teach us to be more open and accepting: seeing the good in people, rather than the bad. And help us to be more honest, able to recognise in ourselves the faults we condemn in others. Amen.

529 Loving God, though we don't like to judge, we need sometimes to make up our minds about people – not to criticise or condemn them, but to assess their motives, gauge their character, and decide upon the sort of person we're dealing with. Teach us to do that wisely, not judging in haste, still less by appearances, nor swayed by hearsay or personal prejudice, but impartial in our approach, awake to the good and bad in everyone, including ourselves. In all our relationships, help us to deal fairly. Amen.

530 Lord Jesus Christ, so often we judge by appearances, taken in by beauty that's skin deep. In our dealings with others, teach us to look beneath the surface to the person beyond. And when it comes to ourselves, may we learn to devote our attention not to outward show but to inner loveliness – to a life that speaks simply of you. Amen.

531 Gracious God, forgive us, for we judge others despite knowing so little about them. Help us to put ourselves in their shoes, learning to see things from their point of view, and, above all, from yours. Amen.

The Lord's Supper

see also Christian seasons: Holy Week

532 Gracious God, weak, wilful and worthless we come to you, knowing that you welcome us, and seek, every moment of every day, to bless us. Faithless, foolish but thankful, we come . . . to be fed, to be filled. Amen.

533 Loving God, we rejoice that, though we consider ourselves unlovely, you consider us precious; though we deserve so little, you delight to give us so much; though we count ourselves sinners, you value us as children; though our faith is weak, your love is strong. So we come, assured of your grace, your goodness, your welcome, through Jesus Christ our Lord. Amen.

534 Lord Jesus Christ, as you requested so we come, in memory of you. Grant that, as we eat and drink together, we may also welcome you into our hearts and receive you into our lives, so that we may remember you in the best way possible: through honouring you in word and deed, and offering faithful service in your name. Amen.

535 Lord Jesus Christ, we share in this meal not in wistful nostalgia or sombre remembrance but joyfully reminding ourselves of the enormity of your love and the awesome sacrifice you made on our behalf. We take bread and drink wine so that we might never forget all you have done, so that your faithfulness might stay fresh in our minds, colouring each moment of every day. Lord Jesus, whatever else we may fail to do, teach us to come in your name and to do this, in memory of you. Amen.

536 Lord Jesus Christ, may the new wine you so freely offer sparkle within us, course through our veins and flow out to others. Amen.

537 Loving God, may the bread of life always nourish us, living water daily refresh us, the broken Christ constantly inspire us and the risen Lord unceasingly guide us. Amen.

538 Bread of life, meet our needs. Broken Christ, heal our wounds. Suffering Saviour, show us mercy. Living Lord, give us life. Amen.

539 May the broken Christ, the poured-out Christ, strengthen us in body, enrich us in mind and nurture us in spirit. Amen.

Love, of God

see also Grace of God

540 Almighty God, thank you, for you created everything that is and has been and ever shall be, yet you have time for each one of us, each person you have made being precious in your eyes. Amen.

541 Gracious God, we put on an act sometimes, pretending to be what we're not. We hide our faults, fears, doubts and sorrows, in case people should think ill of us, seeing these as a sign of weakness. Thank you that, with you, we can be ourselves, for you accept and value us as we are. Teach us to do the same. Amen.

542 Living God, remind us of what it cost you to restore your broken world, the price you so freely paid to make us whole. Remind us of the immensity of your love, the awesome sacrifice through which you have made all things new. We can never repay such goodness, whatever we offer in return, but we give you our praise in grateful thanks and joyful worship. Amen.

543 Redeemer God, thank you for your generous love, never held back or begrudged, but offered liberally, beyond measure – enveloping us, enfolding all. Amen.

544 Mighty and mysterious God, when we gaze at the heavens, the vastness of space and trillions of galaxies, we're overwhelmed, awestruck, even a little afraid, for how can you possibly have time for us, let alone care about our welfare. And yet, amazingly, you *do*! For that astounding truth, thank you. Amen.

545 Lord of all, forgive us, for we see you sometimes as fierce, forbidding, a God to approach with fear and trembling, and we couldn't be more wrong! Amen.

546 Gracious God, thank you for your love, constantly reaching out though we fail to appreciate all you've given or how much it cost you. Thank you that your love and goodness is not dependent on our deserving, but goes on being poured out day after day, generous beyond measure. Amen.

547 Merciful God, thank you that every one of us has a place in your heart, love standing at the centre of our lives and heart of the universe: shaping us, defining *you*. Thank you for so powerfully demonstrating your devotion in Christ, living, dying and rising among us, and for continuing to show it each day, drawing us close despite everything that threatens to pull us apart. Help us to remain as committed to you as you are faithful to us. Amen.

548 Living God, thank you that, for all your awesome power, you are gentle and full of love. Teach us to approach you with confidence, seeing promise instead of threat. Amen.

549 Sovereign God, teach us that you are not stern and forbidding, as some suppose, but gentle and full of love – that, for all your mighty power, you encircle us each day in your loving arms. Amen.

550 Thank you, Lord, that though we hide from you, running from your presence, always you seek us out, never resting until we're found. Amen.

551 Loving God, you know us, every hair of our head, every thought of our mind, every aspect of our character – nothing hidden from your gaze. Inside out and back to front, you know each of us intimately, and yearn that we might know you too. For that great truth, we praise you. Amen.

552 Merciful God, thank you that we can be honest with you and share our deepest secrets – that we have no need to hide the truth, pretending to be what we're not, for you know and love us as we are. Amen.

553 Of your countless gifts, Lord, save us from forgetting the most precious of all: your love in Christ. Amen.

554 Caring God, teach us that we're more than a number to you, more even than just a name; that you value us as individuals, for who and what we are and all that we can be. Remind us that we are unique in your eyes, chosen and precious, and that you willingly paid the ultimate price so that we might know you in person as you know us. Amen.

555 Lord Jesus Christ, thank you for seeing beyond the ugliness of our faults and failings, and glimpsing something of beauty. Teach us, in turn, to look for the best in others, rather than the worst. Amen.

556 Remind us, Lord, that we've no need to pretend, to put on an act or play a part. Teach us that you accept us as we are, and help us to do the same. Amen.

557 Sovereign God, thank you that we can be totally honest with you – that we can open our hearts and bare our souls – since you know and accept us as we are. Help us always to remember that, whatever our weakness, mistakes, doubts or fears, we have no need to hide the truth, pretending to be what we're not, for your love is stronger than all. Amen.

558 All-seeing God, teach us to approach you with confidence rather than hesitancy; to meet and greet you joyfully, knowing that, for all our faults, you accept us as we are. Amen.

559 Lord of all, thank you that we have found a place in your heart – that love stands at the centre of our lives and hub of the universe: shaping us, defining *you*. Amen.

560 Merciful God, teach us that faith isn't about jumping through hoops and somehow gaining your approval, but about receiving what you delight to give; that it doesn't involve performing for you or others, jumping at your command, but is about being the people you created us to be and living life to the full. Help us fully to understand that any conditions to your love are of our making rather than *yours*. Amen.

561 Living God, we grow weary of many things, and not just those that are dull. Familiarity can cause even what we enjoy to lose its lustre, the special coming to seem mundane. Whatever else we grow bored with, however indifferent we may become, may we never tire of you, or the message of your love. Amen.

562 Creator God, teach us that, just as you value the humble sparrow, commonplace though it may be, so you value everything you have made, each of us being special in your eyes. Amen.

563 Faithful God, thank you that wherever we are, wherever we go, your love is with us, to the ends of the earth. Amen.

564 Mighty God, thank you that you are not as people paint you – fierce, frightening, forbidding – but a God of love, dealing tenderly with all. Help us to know you better, so that we may approach you with thanks rather than trepidation, delight instead of disquiet, assured that you are slow to anger, swift to bless and glad to show mercy. Amen.

565 Gracious God, teach us that we have no need to hide from you, for when we go astray you seek us out, not to punish but to bless, not in anger but in love, joyfully carrying us home on your shoulders. Amen.

566 Thank you, Lord, for we have tasted your love and it is good, sweet as honey, a flavour today of heaven tomorrow. Amen.

567 Lord Jesus Christ, though we are worth so little, you were willing to give your all, gladly and without reserve, no price being too high or cost too great to make us yours and you ours. For that awesome truth and amazing love, thank you. Amen.

568 Loving God, thank you that, whoever we are, and whatever we've done, we're not just a number or statistic, but a unique individual, precious in your sight. Amen.

569 Creator God, when we gaze at the heavens, the vastness of space, we're awestruck, moved to praise and worship. But we're also a little afraid, for what we see is just a fraction of the heavens, the merest glimpse of the trillions of galaxies you have made. Compared to the size and antiquity of the universe, how can you possibly have time for us, let alone care about our welfare? And yet, the message of the gospel, the good news made known in Christ, is that amazingly, incredibly, you *do*! For that astounding truth, thank you. Amen.

570 Lord Jesus Christ, thank you, for we were estranged, and you broke down the barriers that kept us apart. You have reached out in love and welcomed us as your friends. Amen.

571 Merciful God, thank you that, whoever we are, whether a model of devotion or black sheep of the family, you value us nonetheless, your love extending to all. Amen.

572 Creator God, thank you that your mighty hand fashioned the universe yet gently encircles us each day, reaching out to hold, to guide and to welcome. Thank you for your power yet tenderness, your infinite might matched by your awesome and unfailing love. Amen.

573 With some we walk on eggshells, Lord, afraid of doing or saying the wrong thing. Thank you that with you it's different, your love accepting us as we are. Amen.

574 Gracious God, thank you for showering us with love, pouring it out day after day, more than we can ever ask or deserve. Help us to love you even a fraction as much in return. Amen.

Love, ours for God

575 Gracious God, forgive us for the insipid service we offer you, looking the part and with so much about it right, yet lacking the one thing needful: the savour of love. Teach us that, in terms of discipleship, the poorest of dishes with that one vital ingredient is worth far more than the finest of feasts without it. Amen.

576 Merciful God, teach us that, however strong our faith or deep our commitment, if love is missing then the rest is flawed, and all the devotion and piety in the world can never redress the balance. Whatever else we lack, then, may your love flow within us – the ground and goal of all our being. Amen.

577 We can't give you much, Lord, still less repay your goodness, but we offer you our love with all our heart. Amen.

578 Faithful God, we like to think that our relationship with you is strong, but when the glue that binds us to you is fear rather than love, superstition rather than faith, or duty rather than joy, then the link is always vulnerable, liable to fail when put to the test. Cement our lives through love, so that the join is firm, able to withstand whatever pressures are put upon it and still to hold fast. Amen.

579 Living God, you weigh our lives in the balance, measuring who and what we are. Teach us to love you better, so that we will not be found wanting. Amen.

Mother's Day

580 Caring and compassionate God, we take you for granted, forgetting the way you hold us in your arms, as a mother cradles her child; the way you teach, provide, comfort and lead, always there when we need you most. Help us to respond, not just today but every day, in grateful and loving service. Amen.

581 Loving God, thank you that whatever life brings, we face it with you, your arms wrapped tight around us, as a mother embraces her child. Amen.

582 Mothering God, we're only children in faith, mere toddlers. Nourish us, and help us to grow. Amen.

Nature and the environment

583 Living God, for all our skill, all our imagination and ingenuity, we cannot fashion anything more special and awesome than the beauty of your creation. Thank you. Amen.

584 Sovereign God, teach us that the skills and ingenuity you have given humankind can either sustain your creation or destroy it. Remind us that the fate of the planet is in our hands, each of us having a part to play. Help us to do our bit faithfully, and grant that others may do the same. Amen.

585 Creator God, for the miracle of life, the wonder of this world and the immeasurable blessings that enrich each day, our hearts leap to you in grateful praise and joyful worship. Amen.

586 Lord of heaven and earth, forgive us, for we have abused your creation, allowing precious resources to disappear down the drain. Teach us to steward your gifts more wisely, remembering it is *your* world, not ours. Amen.

587 Creator God, in the beauty of a flower, and the wonder of spring, speak of your care for us and your love for all. Amen.

588 Eternal God, forgive us, for we're short-sighted, living today with no thought of tomorrow, for ourselves at the cost of others. Remind us of our responsibilities to the wider world – and to you. Amen.

589 Living God, help us to work *with* rather than *against* you – to live in tune with your creation, in harmony with your will and in partnership with others. Instead of squandering your countless gifts or taking your blessings for granted, teach us to consecrate every aspect of life to your service, and to create from it all something beautiful for you. Amen.

590 Creator God, not even the widest of palettes of colour can compare to the one you have used in creation, even the most comprehensive selection being magnified there a million times over: in the splendour of a sunset and magic of a rainbow, the hues of the sea and glory of the sky, the tints of autumn and tapestry of a garden, the plumage of birds and loveliness of a meadow. An immeasurable spectrum brightens every day, causing us to catch our breath in wonder and exult in spirit. For the imprint of your hand on the canvas of life, breathtaking beyond words, receive our praise. Amen.

591 Sovereign God, pardon our folly, for you've created such a beautiful world and too often it passes us by. Teach us to make time to stand and stare. Amen.

592 Lord of heaven and earth, teach us to see in everything you have made, everything around us, a miracle, special beyond words – fashioned by your hands and speaking of you. However ordinary it may seem or familiar be, teach us never to lose our sense of wonder at all you have made. Amen.

593 Creator God, thank you for a world to explore, so full of beauty and with so much to excite, intrigue, enthral and enjoy. Teach us to celebrate all you have given by living each moment to the full. Amen.

594 Living God, thank you for the awesome variety of creation, the breathtaking diversity of life on earth – so much to intrigue, entrance, fascinate and amaze. Teach us to appreciate both the privilege and responsibility it represents, not only rejoicing at all you have given but also respecting its innate worth and dignity and playing our part in protecting it for the future, so that others may marvel in turn. Amen.

595 Sovereign God, thank you for the loveliness of creation, the beauty of this wonderful world – so much around us that gives a taste of heaven here on earth. Amen.

596 Mighty God, thank you for the miracle of life, the wonder of a newborn child, the awesomeness of your creation. Thank you for your *gift* of life, the richness of this world you have given, and health and strength to enjoy it. Thank you for the *new* life you offer in Christ, the rebirth you make possible through him, each day, each moment: a fresh start, full of promise. Living God, receive our praise. Amen.

597 Living God, we've seen it before, so many times, the beauty and wonder of your world, but still we marvel each day at the loveliness of creation, the awesome work of your hands. Amen.

598 Living God, thank you for your artistry in creation: the vibrancy of a rainbow, tints of a sunset, hues of sea, sky, woodland and meadow; the feel of trees, rocks, soil and water; the sound of birds and scent of flowers – the awesome wonder of a world awash with colour, music, flavour and fragrance. Thank you that so much you have made, so much around us, offers a taste of heaven here on earth. Amen.

599 Lord of all, thank you for your creation: the beauty of this world and wonder of the universe. Thank you for so much that speaks of your purpose, causing us to catch our breath in awe and wonder. For the work of your hands and all it reveals of your love, receive our praise. Amen.

600 Sovereign God, through the loveliness of creation, moving us to joy and wonder, open our eyes to things above, captivating beyond words. Amen.

601 Lord of heaven and earth, you've honoured us, each and every one, placing in our care not just land or money but the world itself, an asset beyond price. Forgive our share in squandering its resources, living today with no thought of tomorrow. Forgive our betrayal of your trust, living with little thought for present and future generations. Teach us to live wisely, mindful of all your creation, and grant that others may do the same. Amen.

602 Creator God, you have given us such a beautiful world, able to take away our breath in wonder. Whatever else we have to do, teach us to make time to stop and celebrate. Amen.

New beginnings

see also Confession; Forgiveness; Grace of God; Hope and trust

603 Eternal God, from the dust of the earth you fashioned our bodies and gave us life. And though to the ground we return – dust to dust, ashes to ashes – you promise us new beginnings: love that will neither fade nor perish, a kingdom that never ends. Let us speak, then, not of death and decay, but of your new creation, life for evermore. Amen.

604 Transforming God, help us to see life in death – to look more closely and see the shoots of new birth, new hope, new beginnings. Amen.

605 Gracious God, we make our bed and have to lie on it, or so we're told; but you show us otherwise, offering new beginnings, the chance to start again. For that great truth, we praise you. Amen.

606 Loving God, overhaul our lives, and make us new. Recharge our batteries and clear away whatever prevents us from realising our true potential. So work within us that we may not just get by, but live each moment to the full. Amen.

607 Lord of all, rekindle in us the flame of hope and fire of expectancy, in the knowledge that, with you, however old we might be, life has always only just begun. Amen.

608 Eternal God, we don't like growing older any more than the next person, but though we can disguise the signs of ageing we can never deny them, for they are more than skin deep. Teach us, as *you* do, to accept who we are, and to place into your hands everything we yet might be, recognising that you alone are able to bring true renewal, not just now but for evermore. Amen.

609 Gracious God, we're good at putting on appearances, looking the part, the face we show to the world so often concealing the reality beneath. Help us to change not so much the outside but deep within – to become the people you would have us be. Amen.

610 Loving God, you wash us from within, cleansing the thoughts of the heart, transforming and restoring, offering a fresh start, new beginnings, day after day. Wash us, we pray, in the fountain of your love. Amen.

611 Save us, Lord, from taking you for granted, from assuming we're automatically washed clean, routinely forgiven. Remind us that before we can start again, we must first be truly sorry. Amen.

612 Redeemer God, take the unpromising material of our lives – the unremarkable gifts, commonplace weaknesses, everyday traits and average achievements – and fashion from these all a new person, something special for you. Amen.

613 Mighty God, teach us that small beginnings can lead to surprising results; that what seem like tiny advances can be stepping stones to great achievements and final victory. Amen.

614 Gracious God, thank you for the clean sheet you offer when we make a mess of life; your invitation to turn over a new leaf and start again. Thank you that your mercy is never exhausted, your patience never at an end; that you go on offering new beginnings for as many times as it takes. Amen.

615 Transforming God, thank you that in the darkness of despair, the graveyard of failure, the desert of sorrow, even the shadow of death, your hand is always at work, even when we do not always at first see it. Help us to look more closely, and glimpse in apparent endings the shoots of new beginnings. Amen.

616 Gracious God, thank you that through your coming in Christ you made possible new beginnings – not a superficial change on the outside but real transformation, deep within. Amen.

617 Lord Jesus Christ, we want to be clean, to wash away our mistakes and start again, but, hard though we try, we cannot achieve it alone. Immerse us in your love, and make us new. Amen.

618 We want to be different, Lord, to take off the old self and put on the new, but we strive in vain to change our spots. What we cannot do alone, make possible through your transforming touch. Amen.

619 Merciful God, you offer in Christ a picture of what life can be, what *we* can be – everything made new – yet we struggle to believe it possible, for we fall so far short and find it hard to change even a little. Teach us that, provided we're serious about commitment and prepared to play our part, *you* can do what we can't – fashion a new creation from the incongruous material of our lives. Amen.

New Year

620 God, the same yesterday, today and tomorrow, teach us that though we can remember the past – celebrating and reliving special moments – we can never hold on to it, life moving forwards, not backwards. Help us then to give thanks for all you've done, and eagerly to anticipate what's yet in store. Amen.

621 Faithful God, thank you that in pleasure and pain, triumph and tragedy, hope and fear, health and sickness, you've been with us across another year, leading us safely through its ups and downs, highs and lows. Teach us, recalling your faithful guidance, to trust you for all that lies ahead, knowing that you alone will be the same, yesterday, today and tomorrow. Amen.

622 Lord of past, present and future, we're not so naive as to think everything in this new year will work out as we hope, offering untarnished joy and unbroken fulfilment, for we know well enough life isn't like that, being just as likely to bring tears as laughter and dismay as delight, but teach us, whatever the days ahead may bring, to remember that you will be there by our side, able to lead us from the old to the new, and in all things working together for good. Amen.

One World Week

623 Lord of the nations, when we browse in the shops or fill our basket at the supermarket, speak to us of justice and injustice, trade and commerce, toil and effort, sweat and tears – of the interdependence of humankind and the complex web of life. Remind us each day of what we owe to others, near and far, and the many ways they enrich our lives. Remind us of the breadth and wonder of creation and of our responsibilities towards all. Amen.

624 Lord of all, teach us, through the one made flesh – the one who lived among us, sharing our flesh and blood, knowing our joys and sorrows, experiencing our life and death – to celebrate and honour our common humanity, barriers broken and divisions overcome. Amen.

Patience

see also Stillness and quiet

625 Apologies, Lord, for we're always on your back, asking for more. Help us to be as patient with you as you are with us. Amen.

626 Eternal God, we're not good at waiting. We like to see speedy results, instant returns, and when plans are frustrated, rewards delayed, we fret and sulk. We're not good at waiting for *you* either, growing angry when prayers go unanswered, requests apparently unheeded. Remind us that the best things come to those who wait, and teach us to do things not in our time, but in *yours*. Amen.

627 Eternal God, when we're frustrated by lack of progress, whether in life or faith, teach us to be patient and to take one step at a time, trusting that, slowly but surely, you continue to work within us. Amen.

Peace of God

see also Rest for our souls; Stillness and quiet; Time and space for God

628 Loving God, thank you that we can be at peace, secure in the knowledge that, though *we* sleep, *you* do not. Amen.

629 Lord Jesus Christ, thank you for the peace you promise, not removed from this world, but found amid the hurly-burly of life, the stresses and strains of the daily routine. Open our hearts to that special gift beyond understanding, and may it touch each moment of every day. Amen.

630 Gracious God, thank you for your peace that passes understanding – for the knowledge of your love and assurance of your presence that brings rest to our souls. Amen.

631 Lord, we will lie down in peace and take our rest, for you are with us, for ever by our side. Amen.

Personal response

632 Merciful God, forgive us, for so much of our faith is parroted – imitation commitment, pastiche discipleship – sounding impressive, looking the part, yet in reality borrowed from others, echoing their experiences, using their language, repeating the established jargon, without truly speaking *to* and *for us.* Draw us close to you each day in a deep and vibrant relationship, so that what we say with our lips we may truly believe in our hearts. Amen.

633 Instead of simply toying with faith, help us, Lord, to chew things over – to reflect on who you are, what you say and what you've done, and, meaningfully, to respond. Amen.

634 Living God, in terms of Christian belief we can come up with the right answers, but, unless we've experienced the truth for ourselves, this counts for little. Teach us to know you personally instead of relying on the perception of others; to work *out* our faith and *at* our discipleship, so that it all makes sense for us. Amen.

635 Lord of all, thank you that you are a gentle and loving God, not barking out commands or imposing an iron rule, but inviting a response, calling us to serve of our own free will. Yet, though you do not force us to obey, give us, we pray, the discipline we need – *self*-discipline – to hear your voice and respond, honouring your will and playing our part in the work of your kingdom. Help us to fulfil our responsibilities to you as faithfully as we can. Amen.

636 Gracious God, forgive us, for we mean to respond to you – to acknowledge your goodness, express our gratitude, answer your call – but so often we're found wanting. And whatever excuses we make, they don't hold water, for no concern, however pressing, should be more important than these. Teach us to make time for you as you have made time for us. Amen.

637 Almighty God, forgive us, for we play at faith and toy with discipleship, intrigued and attracted by the message of your love, yet stubbornly keeping you at arm's length. Overcome our reticence, and help us to respond. Amen.

638 Sovereign God, remind us of the true cost of living, and your willingness, through your Son, to pay it. Help us to receive and celebrate the life made possible through him – life in all its fullness – and to give something back in return to you who gave so much. Amen.

639 Living God, save us from judging faith on hearsay, basing our response to you on the opinions of others. Help us personally to investigate the claims of the gospel, and to see for ourselves if they're true – to taste your love firsthand so that we may know beyond doubt how special you really are. Amen.

640 Lord Jesus Christ, remind us that faith involves more than the mind – that, above all, it's an affair of the heart, an adoring response, a relationship of love. Amen.

641 Lord of all, save us from second-hand discipleship, a faith borrowed from others. Instead of judging you on hearsay, help us personally to investigate your claims and to see for ourselves if they're true. Amen.

642 Teach us, Lord, that faith in name only is no faith at all – that in order to be real it needs to be living. Amen.

643 Gracious God, thank you for the knowledge that nothing can ever separate us from your love; for the assurance that, whatever rejection or betrayal you meet with, you will always be faithful to your promises, constant in commitment. Help us to respond in kind, offering you true and passionate devotion. Grant that, instead of being an arid assent with the mind alone, our faith may be a living and loving relationship, for ever made new. Amen.

644 Lord Jesus Christ, we can't give you much, but we offer our love, our service and our faith, consecrating them to you in joyful thanks and heartfelt worship. Amen.

645 Gracious God, you invite us to celebrate your love and share your life, but we're slow to respond, repeatedly putting off our reply. Forgive us, and teach us to answer. Amen.

Power of God

646 Almighty God, teach us never to underestimate your strength, even when it looks like weakness; never to lose sight of the power of love, the might of truth, or the force of good, however much hatred, falsehood or evil may conspire against them. Remind us that nothing in heaven or earth, the present or the future, will finally be able to frustrate your purpose, for you are able to turn sorrow to joy, darkness to light, and death to life – your love being stronger than all. Amen.

647 Sovereign God, thank you that we can place ourselves in your care, knowing that the same hands that fashioned the universe and brought this world into being will encircle us each day, powerful beyond measure yet gentle beyond words. Amen.

648 Thank you, Lord, that when we need support, you are there, a shoulder to lean on in time of trouble, a constant source of strength. Amen.

649 God of all, instead of clinging to money and possessions, as though these are the only support we need, may we hold firmly to you, for you alone can keep us from falling. Amen.

650 Loving God, despite the impression we may give to others, we feel weighed down sometimes by heavy burdens, the pressure building until we feel unable to take the strain any longer. Though *we* can't cope, teach us that *you* can, your strength being sufficient for all our needs. Help us to entrust ourselves into your gracious arms, knowing you will support us, whatever life might bring. Amen.

651 Living God, thank you that though we are weak, you are strong, always there when we need you, to protect, defend and support. Amen.

652 Gracious God, we all carry baggage through life, staggering under a burden of guilt, a weight of remorse, a crushing load of fear. Yet we have no need, for you are ready to carry what we can never shoulder alone. Teach us in turn to let go and walk unencumbered, trusting that you hold everything, even us, in the palm of your hand. Amen.

653 Save us, Lord, from sheepish discipleship, from a feeble and fearful faith. Remind us that you turn expectations upside down, making the strong weak and the weak strong. Amen.

654 Mighty God, thank you that, in a daunting world, you are always there beside us, equipping us for the journey of life. Thank you for the knowledge that though we are weak, *you* are strong. Amen.

655 We're scared, Lord, afraid to confront our fears, but we can't hide away for ever. Teach us to face our demons, knowing you are stronger than all. Amen.

656 Sovereign God, thank you that when we wrestle with heavy loads, weighed down by problems that sap our strength and burdens that crush the spirit, you unfailingly come to our aid, helping to shoulder what we can no longer manage to bear alone. Thank you for being there when we need you most, a constant help in times of trouble. Amen.

657 Mighty God, when we grow weary, drained by the demands and duties of the daily routine, renew our strength and rekindle our zest for life. Amen.

658 Almighty God, we're not in control, no more able to dictate our destiny than to create life or defy death, such a feat being beyond our reach. We can shape things, to a point, exerting influence for better or worse, but more often than not *we're* the one being shaped, swept along by the latest current of opinion or tide of events. Teach us where true power really lies: not in our hands, but in *yours*. Amen.

Practising what we preach

659 Merciful God, forgive us, for sometimes our worship, our service, even our faith is an accessory, an optional extra, put on for show to impress others or simply to make us feel good about ourselves. Help us, rather, to make what we believe part of who and what we are, corresponding with the way we think, speak, act and live. Grant that we may put across a consistent image, not of us, but of you. Amen.

660 Gracious God, have mercy upon us, for though we see sometimes what we believe to be wrong, we keep quiet, afraid to speak out or too lazy to take a stand. For all our talk of lofty ideals we rarely have the courage of our convictions, leaving it instead to others to expose wrongdoing and tackle injustice. Teach us not simply to espouse principles in private but to uphold and defend them, our allegiance plain to all. Amen.

661 Teach us, Lord, that – confronted by evil and injustice – we can't just look the other way, turning our back on the world's ills. Though we can't do much, help us to do *something*. Amen.

662 Lord God, forgive us, for too often we opt for the easy life, a safe, comfortable discipleship that keeps its head down and takes no risks. Remind us that if we would stay true to you, we must be ready sometimes to stick our neck out – to stand up and be counted. Amen.

663 Help us to make a difference, Lord – if not to be salt of the earth, then at least to change something, somewhere, for the better. Help us, through serving others, to serve you. Amen.

664 Merciful God, we know that appearances matter to a point, but you call us to practical commitment rather than ornamental discipleship, to a faith that makes a difference. Save us from showy discipleship that's more froth than substance. Show us what you would have us do and help us to do it, so that we may be not only pleasing in your sight but also useful in your service. Amen.

665 Living God, teach us that rebelliousness has a place in discipleship, that genuine commitment sometimes means questioning the ways of the world and being ready, where necessary, to protest against accepted norms, confronting wrongs and combating evil, however unpopular that may make us. Though we mellow with the years, keep alive the defiance of youth when it comes to standing up for you. Amen.

666 Loving God, we know that words have their place, and an important one too, but help us to balance them with deeds, putting what we say into practice. As well as opening our mouths, teach us to open our hearts. Amen.

667 Gracious God, we make extravagant claims about the way you've changed our lives, the people you've helped us become, and the life you've called us to lead. Forgive us when the walk denies the talk, what people see in us leading them to dismiss the faith we profess as empty hype, more spin than substance. Work within us, so that who we are may more closely resemble who you want us to be. Amen.

668 Almighty God, teach us that though at times we need to stand firm, unyielding on matters of faith and principle, at other times we must be ready to give a little, recognising our limitations, open to new insights and bowing to the wisdom of others. Help us to know which time is which, and give us, as appropriate, the courage or humility to do both. Amen.

669 What impression do we give to others, Lord – above all, what impression of *you*? You call us to imitate Christ, reflecting something of his light and love, but do we get anywhere close to that, or is our discipleship a caricature of what it should be, grotesquely wide of the mark? Though we will always fall short, help us, we pray, to be a little more like Jesus, our lives in some way speaking to others of him. Amen.

Prayer

see also Voice of God

670 Forgive us, Lord, for we treat prayer as a monologue rather than a conversation. Help us to listen, instead of doing all the talking, so that there may be true dialogue between us. Amen.

671 Living God, how long must we call yet find no answer? How long must we seek, yet not find? We call out, but you no longer seem to listen, we look, but cannot see your hand. Help us, for we need your guidance. Hear our prayer. Amen.

672 Gracious God, teach us that staying in touch with you doesn't require special language or a formal approach, but is about a living relationship, making time to share every aspect of life – from the momentous to the mundane, agony to ecstasy, triumphs to tribulations – each shared simply but sincerely in the knowledge that *they* matter to you because *we* matter. Amen.

673 Father God, teach us that not everything comes gift-wrapped, that some things in life must be worked for. Remind us then, when prayers seem unanswered and hopes go unrealised, that instead of being *your* fault it might be *ours*, the fulfilment of our requests lying not in greater faith but in greater effort! Amen.

674 Lord Jesus Christ, thank you that we can bring you our deepest needs, our inner yearning for meaning and purpose, confident that, when we ask in faith, you will hear and answer. Amen.

675 Mighty and mysterious God, we don't know how prayer works, how you hear or speak, how our messages can possibly get through, yet, like generations before us, we have heard your voice and sensed your presence, discovering for ourselves that you listen and respond. Though the mechanics are beyond us, teach us to treasure your gift of prayer, and to use it. Amen.

676 Lord of all, when we call to you yet nothing seems to happen, when we ask for help and guidance, yet seem to wait in vain, give us patience – wisdom to trust in *your* timing rather than our own. Amen.

677 Father God, you have given us prayer so that we can share our needs, seek your help and hear your voice. Forgive our failure to use it. Amen.

Pressure, when feeling under

see also Trouble, help in times of

678 Almighty God, we're not as strong as we like to think, the burdens of life sometimes being too heavy to bear. Thank you that when we cannot carry them alone, you are always there to share the load, nothing being too hard for you to shoulder. Amen.

679 Living God, we feel drained sometimes, fit for nothing, reserves run dry. Yet you are a God of power, revitalising the spirit, renewing strength. Flow into our hearts, and out through our lives. Amen.

680 Mighty God, when work piles up, weighing heavily upon us, give us wisdom to take things one step at a time, lest we collapse under the weight of it all and end up achieving nothing. Amen.

681 Lord Jesus Christ, when we're drained by the demands placed upon us, wearied to the point of exhaustion, renew our strength, and help us to go the extra mile. Amen.

682 Mighty God, thank you that when we're weary, the load too heavy to bear, you carry not just the burden, but us as well. Amen.

683 Father God, when we're at the end of our tether, our patience stretched to the limit, give us wisdom to recognise our limitations and grace to accept the constraints life puts upon us, before we reach breaking point and something snaps. Amen.

684 We're tired, Lord, exhausted by the pressures of life, the daily demands that are placed upon us. Renew our strength, and help us to get through. Amen.

Purpose of God

685 Eternal God, remind us that, whatever moves we make, however carefully we plan, we don't have all the answers. Help us to live wisely in the present and to trust finally in your future. Amen.

686 Lord of all, forgive us, for we expect you to pander to our every whim, as though faith is all about us rather than *you*, and, of course, we've failed to get the picture, misunderstood things completely. Teach us to seek your will, rather than expecting you to conform to our own. Amen.

687 Gracious God, so much in our lives obstructs your purpose and prevents you from working as you would. Though we like to think we are growing in faith, the truth is that you are still preparing the ground, making ready the foundations. Clear away everything that hampers your will, so that you can truly build us up and finish your new creation. Amen.

688 God of yesterday, today and tomorrow, so often we can see the beginning of things, but not the end, and we wonder sometimes where life may lead. Teach us to take each moment as it comes, and to leave the future to you. Amen.

689 Loving God, without you we struggle to find the right direction, being less than straight in our dealings with others, hesitant in following our intended course, unable to draw a line under the past, incapable of measuring up to the call of Christ. Open our hearts to the height, length, breadth and depth of your loving purpose, and may that yardstick bring new dimensions to life and a proper perspective on all we do. Amen.

Questions of faith

690 Another disaster, another tragedy, another tale of sorrow and suffering. Where were you, Lord, when it happened? What were you thinking of? How could you let it be? We look for answers, yet search in vain, the quest raising more questions than it solves, but if one thing is clear, it's that here, in this time of crisis, we need you more than ever. Come to our broken, bleeding world and bind up its wounds. Assure us, despite how things seem, that hope is mightier than fear, right stronger than wrong, and love greater than all. Amen.

691 Are you out there, Lord? We want to believe it, *try* to believe it, yet at times we look for you in vain. Give us a clearer glimpse of your presence beyond. Amen.

692 Almighty God, for some reason questions about you are discouraged, as though we either shouldn't have any or should know all the answers. Yet if, even in small things, we have gaps in our knowledge, how much more so must it be when it comes to you? Teach us, recognising your greatness and the limitations of our understanding, to ask honestly and openly about matters of faith, conscious that, however much we have grasped, there is always far more still to learn. Amen.

693 Give us enquiring minds, Lord, open to new ideas and eager to think them through. Help us to look, to listen, and to understand. Amen.

694 Mighty and mysterious God, it's hard sometimes not to dismiss you as fantasy, for though we speak of your strength and protection, in so many situations of human need you seem strangely absent. Evil prospers while the good suffer, our cries for help seemingly passing unheeded. In all the paradoxes of this life, help us to keep faith that, one day, your will shall be done and your kingdom come. Amen.

695 Gracious God, can't you control this world you've made, putting an end to its hatred, sorrow, pain and death? Can't you turn war to peace, evil to good, sickness to health and darkness to light, all at the touch of your hand? But that's the wrong question, isn't it, for you *can* and *do* change things, only not remotely but by consent, not *controlling* what we do but *inviting* our response. And though the price can be high, we wouldn't have it any other way, for we'd much rather be a unique individual than a puppet. Thank you for freedom to choose, and teach us to use it wisely. Amen.

696 Almighty God, so much in life is hard to fathom, leaving us troubled and confused, unable to reconcile it with your love. We struggle to take in the mysterious ways in which you work and the sheer breadth of your purpose, our faith foundering as a result. Teach us to celebrate what we *can* make sense of, and to trust you in what we *can't*. Amen.

697 Loving God, thank you, for you have shone into our hearts – breaking through the darkness of doubt and disbelief – and helped us to see the light. Amen.

698 Lord of all, we don't find faith easy, for so much in life fails to make sense, seeming to deny your love. In a world full of mystery, help us to live with questions. Amen.

699 We see much, Lord, but understand little, so much in life being a puzzle, hard to reconcile with faith in your loving purpose. Help us to work through our questions, patiently, humbly and openly, and grant that they may lead us finally into a fuller understanding of your will, a greater sense of your goodness and a deeper awareness of your grace. Amen.

700 Living God, we struggle sometimes to make sense of life or to extricate ourselves from the tangled web we weave. We search for answers to our questions and solutions to our problems, but the harder we try to disentangle the loose ends, the more tightly we tie ourselves in knots. Meet us in our confusion, and draw the jumbled threads of our lives together. Entwine us with the cords of your love, creating there, and there alone, a bond that can never be loosened. Amen.

701 We try to believe, Lord, but it's not easy, life throwing up so many questions and so few answers. Increase our faith, and bear with our doubt. Amen.

702 Father God, we try to work things out, to find solutions to our problems, but time and again we come unstuck, life failing to conform to our calculations. Teach us to trust in *you* in whom alone lies the answer to all. Amen.

703 Lord of all, we walk a fine line between faith and doubt, belief and unbelief, our commitment being less secure than we like to pretend. Deepen our trust in you, so that we may be equipped to meet whatever challenges life throws at us and still stand firm. Teach us that we need to be open to questions if faith is to grow, but must also recognise the limitations of what we can understand, and help us to get the balance right. Amen.

704 When we look at the world, Lord – its tensions and suffering, need and heartbreak – it's hard not to wonder what you're doing and why you take so long to put things right, for so much within it seems to question your love and undermine your will. Help us to understand, though, that there are no quick fixes or short-term solutions, but that you are working nonetheless, your purpose destined finally to triumph, not in our time but in *yours*. Amen.

705 Creator God, why did you fashion a world so awesome yet so awful, enriched by joy yet cursed by sorrow; a world in which so much speaks of your care, but so much else denies it, giving your love the lie? Help us to wrestle honestly with the good and the bad, the best and the worst in life, and somehow to make sense of you in each. Amen.

706 Mighty God, your ways are beyond us, too hard to understand, yet you continue to work, day after day, and that's all we need to know. Amen.

Relationships

see also Intercession: For peace and harmony; Judging others; Worth of all

707 Lord of all, forgive us for failing to appreciate our loved ones, slow not simply to show our gratitude but even to notice the innumerable ways they enrich our lives. Teach us to recognise everything they do, and, in word and deed, to show how much it means. Amen.

708 Father God, give us wisdom in our dealings with others, sensitivity to their feelings, so that we may learn to tread carefully where we might otherwise cause offence. Instead of acting in ways that upset or goad people, like a red rag to a bull, help us to avoid unnecessary confrontation, seeking instead the way of peace. Amen.

709 Have mercy, Lord, for too often we open our big mouths, and wish we hadn't, our words serving to hinder instead of help. In all our relationships, teach us when to speak and when to keep silent. Amen.

710 Living God, help us to put ourselves into the shoes of those around us – not literally, but in spirit – for only then can we hope to understand them, to grasp what makes them tick and make sense of their experiences, empathising with their hopes and fears, joys and sorrows. Teach us to look beyond our limited horizons and narrow interests, and to identify more fully with others, as you have identified yourself so wonderfully with us and with all. Amen.

711 Gentle and generous God, forgive us, for too easily we allow our temper to overheat, and though there are many reasons, it's finally down to us, our neglect of you and failure to grow in grace. Fill us with gentleness, patience and self-control, so that should steam start to rise, you may channel it safely and help us to cool off, before *all* pay the price. Amen.

712 Lord Jesus Christ, however unpalatable it may be, however hard to stomach, when we need to swallow our pride, give us courage to do so. Amen.

713 Lord of all, forgive us, for too easily we pigeonhole people, boxing them into categories that say more about us than about them. Overcome the prejudices that lurk within us, and help us to see beyond our preconceptions. Amen.

714 Father God, however different others may be, however less like us they may seem, teach us to look beyond prejudice and stereotypes and to approach all with an open mind. Amen.

715 In all our relationships, Lord, help us to hit the right note. Keep us in tune with you, and, where possible, in harmony with others. Amen.

716 Gracious God, in many things, more than we realise, our pleasure comes at the expense of others, what brings us joy causing them pain. Teach us, in all we do, however innocent it may seem, to consider its impact on those around us, and, where necessary, to put their wishes before our own. Amen.

717 Lord Jesus Christ, forgive us, for we can cause discord more easily than we imagine, clashing with those around us and even with you. In all our relationships, help us to hit the right note; to be in tune with you, and, wherever possible, to live in harmony with others. Amen.

718 It's easy to tear down, Lord – we do it all the time. Through a harsh word or critical look we rip the ground from beneath people's feet, undermining their confidence and demolishing their self-esteem. Living Lord, forgive us for finding fault, magnifying weaknesses and dwelling on mistakes, and instead of putting people down, help us to build them up – constructive in all we do, think and say. Amen.

719 Loving God, when we focus too much on personal goals and ambitions, teach us to think also of others, and, where necessary, to put their interests before our own. Give us the humility we need to take a back seat sometimes; to play a supporting part and let others enjoy their moment. Amen.

720 Forgive us, Lord, for we turn our back on others, forgetting that we need *them* and *they* need us. Teach us that we belong together. Amen.

721 Father God, like everyone else we're instinctively attracted to those of like mind, resisting those who differ. But though we know it's natural, we know also it's wrong, for we need people of opposite ideas and contrasting experiences to bring balance to our lives, countering our lopsided view of the world and making up what we lack. However hard we find it to get on with some people, inspire us to see beyond what pushes us apart to what draws us together. Amen.

722 Teach us that the hurt people cause is not always intended, so much of what they say and do being an instinctive response rather than premeditated. Help us, then, when our instinct is to lash out and hurt in turn, to bear the wounds with grace, remembering how you so willingly were wounded for all in Christ. Amen.

723 God of grace, thank you for the company of others, all who enrich each day simply by being there. Reach out to those who have no one, and in their loneliness be there for *them*. Amen.

724 Father God, too often we find fault for little reason, swift to condemn and slow to praise. We focus on weaknesses rather than strengths, faults instead of virtues, failure instead of success; the negatives swamping the positives until we can see nothing else. Forgive us, and instead of dwelling on the worst in people, help us to see the best. Amen.

725 Living God, we build barriers that keep us from others – walls of fear, resentment, pride and envy. Forgive us, and help us to break them down. Amen.

726 Loving God, we don't know when to stop sometimes. Whether it's flogging a joke, testing someone's patience, taking liberties or indulging to excess, we can push things too far and, though we may not see it, damage is done, greater than we might imagine. Whatever we start, help us to know when it's time to call a halt. Amen.

727 Lord of all, teach us that we need others – that you created us not to exist in isolation but to enjoy company, interacting with those around us. Cement, then, the ties of friendship, and build up the relationships we share, for it is so often through these that you give shape and purpose to life. Amen.

728 Lord of all, we get angry sometimes with so little cause. Silly things, trivial, incidental, get us ludicrously worked up until sparks fly and we, so to speak, blow a fuse – only it pops too late, the explosion of energy wreaking havoc before it is spent, potentially scarring for life. Teach us, when anger takes hold, to trip the switch before the damage is done. Amen.

729 Gracious God, thank you that we are all different, each having something unique to give and receive, teach and learn. Help us to celebrate and respect that variety, so that it may enrich rather than estrange, unite instead of divide. Amen.

730 Too easily, Lord, we're swayed by appearances, by beauty that's skin-deep. Teach us, with all we meet, to look beyond outward show to the person underneath. Amen.

731 Lord Jesus Christ, forgive us, for we're suspicious of differences, interpreting them as threat instead of promise, reason to fear rather than celebrate. Overcome what divides us from others, and make us one. Amen.

732 Lord Jesus Christ, teach us that we should simmer with rage about some things in life – injustice, exploitation, greed, hatred and violence – but remind us also how easily anger can spill over into rage, destroying and wounding, adding to rather than alleviating the world's misery. Show us when it's right to be angry, but help us always to channel it, so that it will be a tool for good instead of evil. Amen.

733 Loving God, remind us that what's to our taste doesn't necessarily appeal to others; that what's right for us isn't always right for all. Teach us to respect people's entitlement to choose, instead of forcing our preferences upon them. Amen.

734 Living God, we need the company of others to remove rough edges, the experience of rubbing shoulders with people of different backgrounds, ideas and experiences if we're to become fully rounded. Open our hearts to others and, through our bouncing off them, shape our lives for good. Amen.

735 Loving Lord, thank you that with you there are no insiders and outsiders – those you love and those you don't – your concern being for all. Give us similar openness of mind and the same generosity of spirit. Amen.

736 Gracious God, we try to avoid the mistake of pride, but just occasionally we preen ourselves in public – smug about some achievement or self-satisfied about a virtuous deed – and there are times when, subconsciously, despite our best intentions we disparage others, assuming our way, understanding or motives are better than theirs. Forgive us and help us to follow the pattern of Christ, remembering that he, though greater than all, counted himself as nothing, emptying himself to the point of death in order to raise us to life. Teach us, then, to count others better than ourselves, looking to their interests before our own. Amen.

737 Gracious God, teach us to look behind the labels, especially when it comes to people, recognising that the terms so often used – East, West, black, white, Christian, Muslim, liberal, extremist – can only tell part of the story, never the whole. Help us, in all our dealings with others, to see the person first and the label second. Amen.

738 Loving God, we'd never hurt anyone on purpose, yet we *do* hurt them, too many times to number, wounding the spirit if not the body. A foolish comment here, thoughtless deed there, and before we know it the harm is done – what seems innocuous capable of wreaking havoc. Save us from hasty words and careless actions, and in all we say or do teach us to consider others, and you. Amen.

739 Teach us, Lord, to recognise our strengths and weaknesses, those things we're made for and those we're not, and teach us equally to respect the qualities of others, being open to what *they* can do that *we* can't. Amen.

740 Father God, you do not expect us always to be in concert with others, in unison with their every whim and wish, for there are times when faithful discipleship entails singing to a different tune, and clashes are inevitable, but help us to avoid what inevitably leads to discord: pride, hatred, deceit, envy, selfishness, anger, greed. Help us to strike the right note at the right time, as far as possible living harmoniously with all. Amen.

741 Loving God, just as you came in Christ to reconcile the world to yourself, come again now and reach out to all whose relationships are broken, undermined by mistakes and misunderstanding, and, through your healing touch, rekindle love. Put an end to our petty divisions, and bring back together those whom life has pushed apart. Amen.

742 Lord of all, remind us that what we see of others is rarely the whole story; that behind the façade, beneath the veneer, most of them wrestle with their secret pain, hidden fears and inner turmoil – casualties of the hurly-burly of life. Teach us that beneath the public face there lies a private world, and help us in all our dealings to allow for both. Amen.

743 Lord Jesus Christ, teach us, wherever and whenever we can, to be peacemakers, not poking our nose in where it's not wanted, but ready, when we find ourselves caught in the middle of discord, to serve as a go-between, mediating your love. Give us, then, sensitivity to calm the waters, wisdom to break the deadlock and love to heal the wounds. Amen.

744 Living God, save us from a second-hand existence; from spending too much time watching other people's lives and not enough living our own. Amen.

745 Save us, Lord, from being so full of our own importance, so sure of our rightness, that we refuse to see another's point of view. Help us to climb down when we're wrong. Amen.

746 Lord Jesus Christ, should we fall out with others, give us grace to admit our faults, humility to say sorry, and resolve to make amends. Amen.

747 Creator God, teach us in the world of everyday life and relationships, to work in partnership with you, seeking to nurture the full potential of everyone and everything. Amen.

748 Loving God, remind us that differences need not divide; that, however unlikely it may seem, you can draw all people together, and truly make them one. Amen.

749 Teach us, Lord, that it takes all sorts to make a world – that each one of us is different, special, unique in your eyes. Help us to see the best in everyone, as you see the best in us. Amen.

750 Loving God, thank you for friends and family, all who brighten each day by their presence, who give meaning to life and help to make us what we are. Amen.

751 Father God, too often we're clumsy in our dealings with others, coming down forcefully on little things when a quiet word would suffice, hopelessly heavy-handed when a light touch is all that's needed. Teach us, if we would foster rather than shatter the spirit, to think fairly, love deeply and deal gently in all we do. Amen.

752 Lord of all, we like to think that we're friendly, receptive and welcoming, even to outsiders . . . but we're not. All too often the shutters go up when our view of the world is questioned – our minds being closed to customs and convictions that threaten our own. Forgive us, and teach us, instead of automatically locking the door, to open it to others, recognising that you speak through their words, challenge through their insights and meet us through their presence. Amen.

753 Lord Jesus Christ, though we're scared of what it might lead to, afraid it may bounce back in our face, help us to love our enemies and to make the first move towards restoring peace. Amen.

754 Living God, what message do our lives give to others, and what do they say of you? Are we open to people or closed, as approachable as we like to think or aloof, even dismissive? Break down the walls we erect – the barriers of prejudice, fear, pride and suspicion – so that our lives may reflect your love and openness to all. Amen.

755 Whatever our troubles, Lord, whatever our problems or worries, may we never be so wrapped up in ourselves that we've no time to comfort another. Amen.

756 Almighty God, when we give ourselves airs and graces, thinking of ourselves more highly than we should, remind us of how small we truly are, and teach us to walk humbly with you and with others. Amen.

757 Lord Jesus Christ, when we've spoken or acted unkindly, help us not simply to kiss and make up, but to recognise our faults, and rather than trying to change *others*, to change ourselves instead. Amen.

758 Merciful God, whether we're at fault or otherwise, teach us when tempers fray and relationships are soured to swallow our pride and make the first overtures towards reconciliation. Amen.

Remembrance Day

see also Intercession: For peace and harmony

759 Father God, remind us, lest we forget, of the debt we owe – the life made possible through the death of others. Help us to cherish and nurture the things they died for – liberty, justice and peace – so that their sacrifice will not have been in vain. Amen.

760 Living God, teach us truly to appreciate the freedom we enjoy and never to forget what it cost so many. Remind us of the awfulness of conflict, so that we might strive always for peace. And awaken us to our part in a broken world and our responsibility to work for its healing. Amen.

Rest for our souls

see also Peace of God; Stillness and quiet

761 Father God, thank you, for we were heavy laden, weighed down by daily demands and duties, and you saw our need, helping us to bear what we could not carry alone. Thank you that we can cast our cares on to you and find rest for our souls. Amen.

762 Thank you, Lord, that however weary we may grow, you never tire, continuing to watch over us day and night. Thank you that we can rest easy, our minds at peace, secure in the knowledge that, though *we* sleep, *you* do not. Amen.

763 Gracious God, whether we sleep or are awake, thank you that you are always there, a constant companion, daily strength, and faithful friend. Thank you that the peace you make possible is unlike anything the world can give, bringing inner stillness, quiet assurance, rest for our souls. Amen.

Seeking and finding

see also Wisdom, seeking

764 Give us an enquiring mind, Lord: an innate curiosity to learn about you and to know you better. However much we've understood, remind us that faith constantly needs to explore fresh horizons, delving into the riches of who and what you are. We've glimpsed a little: help us to see more. Amen.

765 Lord Jesus Christ, teach us that your call to seek and find is not a one-off instruction – advice we can act on once and then forget about – but an indispensable guideline for discipleship, to be persevered with throughout the journey of faith. Help us, then, to search patiently for greater understanding, deeper commitment and a fuller love for you and others, assured that if we truly seek such things, we *will* find. Amen.

766 Father God, thank you, for we were weighed down and you gave us rest. Help us in turn to bear the burdens of others, or at least to lighten their load. Amen.

767 Living God, when we call to you but find no answer, when we seek for your presence, but search in vain, teach us to look more closely until we find. Amen.

768 Mighty and mysterious God, when we're tempted to settle for superficial faith, teach us to dig deeper, searching always for fresh insights, food to nourish our souls. Assured that those who seek *will* find, may we hammer away in faith, each day bringing us greater knowledge of your love, your will and your truth, satisfying deep within. Amen.

Service

769 Are we doing enough, Lord – as much as we imagine – or are we simply making excuses, putting off what we'd rather not face? Help us truly to serve you, not doing as little as we can get away with but going the extra mile, giving and giving again to you who gave your all for us. Amen.

770 Living God, the tasks you call us to may not be glamorous, catching the eye or earning the plaudits, but they are no less necessary for that, for so often it is those in the shadows who are the unsung heroes, support staff who make possible the star roles. Grant us, then, humility to serve in whatever way you ask, and to appreciate the ways *others* serve *us*. Amen.

771 Lord Jesus Christ, we get carried away sometimes, so concerned with things above that we lose touch with earth below. Help us to keep our feet on the ground, and to serve you in the here and now. Amen.

772 Father God, whatever you call us to, whether a position in the limelight or doing the donkey work behind the scenes, help us to fulfil our role gladly, content to play our part faithfully in your service. Amen.

Stillness and quiet

see also Peace of God; Rest for our souls; Time and space for God

773 Loving God, by day as well as by night our spirit is all too often restless, unable to find true fulfilment or inner tranquillity. Help us to let go of our fears, and to place every part of life into your hands, so that we may know the rest you promise and find true contentment – a quietness of body, mind and soul that, day or night, cannot be shaken. Amen.

774 Almighty God, in quiet reverence and grateful worship we kneel before you, seeking a deeper sense of your presence. In the stillness, help us to know that you are God. Amen.

775 God of past, present and future, teach us that life is not a race, a battle to beat the clock. Help us to live each moment as it comes, celebrating the day you have made, and remembering that time itself is in your hands. Amen.

776 Father God, help us, for we're always in a hurry, rushing madly from one thing to the next. Teach us that life is not a race, a battle to beat the clock, but a gift, a journey of discovery, a foretaste of eternity. Help us, then, to live each moment as it comes, celebrating the day you have made, and remembering that time itself is in your hands. Amen.

777 Creator God, teach us to appreciate the simple but special things of life, to make time each day, if only for a moment, to stop and stare, and to celebrate the beauty of all you have made. Amen.

778 Lord of all, teach us, whatever else needs doing, to make time to unwind and hear your voice, to be still and glimpse your presence. Save us from being so concerned with the daily demands of life that we have no time left truly to live. Amen.

779 Father God, teach us to take things more gently, matching our pace with yours instead of hurrying from one thing to the next. Teach us that it is better sometimes to make haste slowly than to rush headlong into a new venture and then regret it afterwards. Teach us the secret of patience – the ability to trust in your timing, recognising that the journey can be as special as the destination. Amen.

780 Loving God, though you promise shelter when the wind blows, a haven in times of turmoil, save us from divorcing faith from life, as though commitment involves running away from the world and the challenges it brings. May moments of retreat and quiet devotion inspire us rather to fresh service and new ventures in faith. Amen.

781 Living God, teach us, however busy we may be, that we need sometimes to stop and relax; that if we're to function as effectively as we would wish and stay healthy in mind, body and spirit, we need to make time not just for our daily duties, nor even just for you, but also for ourselves. Give us strength for whatever we're asked to take on, but wisdom also to know when to stop. Amen.

782 Creator God, thank you for green spaces – meadows, parks, gardens, countryside – everywhere that we can roam free, escaping the noise of traffic, the concrete jungle, the daily routine. Thank you for places where we can relax and reflect, in tune with nature, with ourselves and with you. Amen.

783 Eternal God, the older we get, the more it feels as though the stopwatch is ticking and time is running out, so we rush around from one thing to the next determined to cram ever more into the unforgiving minute. Yet so easily, in our haste, we forget to enjoy what we have, to let go of striving and simply to live. Remind us that though this mortal span may be slipping away, it is just a taste of things to come; that though the days are passing, we have no cause to fret, for with you we have all the time in the world . . . and far, far beyond! Amen.

784 Father God, we forget that we need to switch off sometimes if we're not to end up exhausted. Teach us to appreciate the importance of being still, of taking a breather from the demands of life, however pressing they may be. Show us the difference between doing enough and doing too much, and help us to get the balance right. Amen.

785 We need to relax, Lord, but there's so much still to do. Help us to let go, so that, truly refreshed, we may do it better. Amen.

786 Loving God, thank you for moments to let go; to forget, if only briefly, the demands and duties of each day. Thank you for opportunities to unwind and to celebrate the sheer joy of being alive. Teach us, whatever else we do, to make time and space in our lives – for us, for others and for you. Amen.

787 God of past, present and future, when we grow impatient, fretting about being made to wait; when we race around at breakneck speed, furiously striving to cram as much as possible into every day; when we begrudge a wasted hour or unfilled minute; teach us to slow down and to take things one step at a time. Whatever we need to do, whatever we *want* to do, may we recognise first what we *can* and what we *can't* do, and appreciate the difference. Help us always to celebrate the given moment rather than brood over the next or the last. Amen.

788 Gracious God, remind us that we need to pause sometimes if we're to make sense of life, time to stop and stare being essential if we're to keep things in balance and live as you intend. In the many demands and duties we face each day, teach us to make space for stillness and quiet – space for us and for you. Amen.

789 Thank you, Lord, for moments to relax, to forget for a time the cares of the world, the demands and duties that cling so closely, and simply to unwind, celebrating the sheer joy of being alive. Amen.

790 Why, Lord, do we habitually rush through life? Why are we forever in a hurry? Grant us the gift of patience and the ability to celebrate each moment, whatever it may bring. Teach us to savour the here and now, and to let go of what might be or could have been. Amen.

Time and space for God

see also Stillness and quiet

791 Eternal God, forgive us, for too easily we forget you, repeatedly overlooking your presence, and failing even – sometimes for days on end – to give you a second thought. Teach us what matters most in life – your love, your will, your grace, your goodness – and whatever else we may forget, may we remember *you*. Amen.

792 Lord of all, help us to focus on you, to concentrate our thoughts in daily devotion and faithful discipleship, making you the centre of all we do and are, the hub of our lives and goal of our being. Whatever temptations and pressures we face, may nothing distract us from knowing you better and responding in grateful, loving service. Amen.

793 In the routine of a busy day, Lord, with so much clamouring for our attention, teach us to pause and ponder – to make time for you. Amen.

794 Eternal God, despite our rushing round in circles, we could achieve far more if only we were to get our priorities right and focus on the things that matter. So little of what we do is as pressing as we like to think and so much gets us nowhere. Teach us to make time – for us, for others and for you. Amen.

795 We try to pray, Lord, but we're so easily distracted. Teach us to shut out what's unimportant, and to focus on you. Amen.

Trouble, help in times of

see also Faithfulness of God; Pressure, when feeling under

796 Lord Jesus Christ, for being there for us, whenever we need you, a shoulder to lean on, a friend in need, thank you. Amen.

797 Thank you, Lord, for we were in a corner, up against the wall, and you came to help – a rescuer in time of need. Amen.

798 Father God, forgive us, for we repeatedly lose our sense of perspective. We turn minor weaknesses into major faults, disappointments into tragedies, and problems into crises, trivial disputes blown up into blazing rows and innocent remarks taken as personal slights. Help us to see things as they really are. Amen.

799 Help us, Lord, for we get ourselves into such a mess, seemingly unable to help ourselves. Lift us out of the mire, and enable us to start again. Amen.

800 Loving God, in a dark and dangerous world, guard us in body, mind and soul. Lead us away from temptation and deliver us from evil. Amen.

801 Lord of all, anchor our lives in your love, your word, your will, so that we may be able to resist the trials life throws at us. Nurture our faith and strengthen our commitment, so that, whatever turmoil we face, whatever testing we endure, when all has done its worst we may still stand tall – unbowed, unbroken. Amen.

802 Father God, thank you, for whatever we're up against, however tight our predicament, you come to our aid and show us the way out. Amen.

803 Help us, Lord, for we're in trouble and don't know where to turn. Hear our cry, and rescue us before we fall. Amen.

804 Gracious God, even when it's hard, everything seeming to count against it, teach us to keep faith, knowing that, however much we falter and however hard we fall, you will lift us up and set us back on our way. Amen.

805 Eternal God, thank you that in a world of change, you are our rock; that in a world of uncertainty, you are solid ground beneath our feet; that in a world of danger, you are our refuge. Thank you that, wherever life's journey takes us, you are always there, our strength and salvation in time of need. Amen.

806 We're so small, Lord, and life's dangers are so huge. Protect us, and keep us safe. Amen.

807 Lord God, help us, for we're stuck and don't know what to do. Come to our aid and rescue us, for we can't hold on much longer. Amen.

808 Father God, so easily lives are ruined by the trials and tribulations of life, bitterness destroying what might have been, curdling the milk of human kindness, souring relationships, turning rancid what once brought joy. Whatever hurts or disappointments we face, help us to deal with them and move on, lest in making a meal of them, they end up making a meal of us. Amen.

809 What can we do, Lord? Where can we turn? Trouble has struck, and there's no one to help. You alone are our strength and support. Be there to see us through. Amen.

810 Loving God, help us to keep on bouncing back, however hard or far we fall. May we leap up from life's trials and disappointments with increased vigour, renewed in body, mind and spirit. May we reach closer to you, scaling fresh heights in faith, until our hands meet and heaven touches earth. Amen.

811 Mighty God, thank you that in the storms of life, when we sometimes feel helpless and alone, unsure what the future may hold, you are always there to guide, protect and save. Teach us to put our trust in you, come wind, come weather, assured that you will see us through this life to our journey's end. Amen.

812 Loving God, when life brings troubles – stretching our resources, sapping our strength and testing us to the limit – give us a bulldog spirit, a faith that will not give in but perseveres to the end. Amen.

813 Living God, sometimes we feel knocked about by forces beyond our control, battered this way and that by circumstances until, finally, we can take the punishment no longer. Yet you promise strength to the weary and support to the faint; to see us through however fierce the testing. In the chaos and confusion of life we put our trust in you. Amen.

814 When troubles throw us off balance, Lord, taking our feet from under us, be there to give support and set us straight once more. Amen.

815 When we're tired out, wearied to the point of exhaustion, restore our strength, and revive our flagging spirit. Amen.

816 Thank you, Lord, for we were going under, battered by the storms of life, but you reached out to save, and rescued us from the waves. Amen.

817 Gracious God, help us, to glimpse your light even when life is at its darkest. Though the night of sorrow, fear, pain or doubt closes in, cold and forbidding, may a glimmer of your love shine through – a glimpse of your presence sufficient to sustain faith, nourish hope and impart peace. Amen.

818 Lord Jesus Christ, when troubles turn life sour, leaving a nasty taste in the mouth or threatening the goals we've worked for, save us from resentment or self-pity, from growing bitter too. Help us to trust in your transforming touch, able to work in all things for good. Amen.

819 Father God, support us when our mood is black, life seeming dark beyond redemption. Though we feel hopelessly lost – unsure where to turn next, unsure of everything – teach us that there is always light at the end of the tunnel and that your love will guide us to it. Amen.

820 Thank you, Lord, for time and again, and in all kinds of ways, you've come to our aid and delivered us. Amen.

821 Loving God, remind us, in the storms of life, when the clouds hang heavy and the world seems dark, that your light continues to shine though all seems in turmoil. Teach us, however distant you may seem, still to trust you, assured that your love will break through and its radiance enfold us once more. Amen.

822 Lord Jesus Christ, thank you that when we reach out, seeking your help in time of need, you are always there, ready to help, to heal and to hold. Amen.

823 Rescue us, Lord, for we're up to our neck in trouble and cannot hold on much longer. Come to our aid and lift our head above the waves. In you alone lies our hope. Reach out and deliver us from the storm. Amen.

824 Redeemer God, sometimes life brings us down to earth with a bump – dreams shattered, plans frustrated, happiness destroyed. Help us at such times, instead of feeling sorry for ourselves and cursing our luck, to pick ourselves up and start again, knowing that there is no gain without pain, no joy without sorrow, no laughter without tears. However often we may fall, renew our trust, in life and in you. Amen.

825 Though danger threatens, Lord, and trouble is near, teach us that we have nothing to fear, for whatever may harm the body, it cannot touch the soul. Amen.

826 Merciful God, repeatedly, in time of trouble, you have stretched out your hand and provided for our needs. For the constancy of your care, thank you. Amen.

827 Father God, though faith cannot insulate us from the blows of life or protect us from being hurt, thank you for being there to comfort, ready to mend our broken hearts and wipe away the tears. Thank you that, in sickness or in health, joy or sorrow, your arms continue to enfold us, eternity itself held in your embrace. Teach us to trust in you and to find peace in your outstretched arms. Amen.

828 We thought we were in control, Lord, life going according to plan, but suddenly we're tied up in knots and can see no way out. Help us to sort out this mess, before we're overwhelmed completely. Amen.

829 Gracious God, we were sinking, up to our neck in problems and about to go under, but you heard our cry and rescued us. Thank you. Amen.

830 We're in trouble, Lord, *big* trouble, and we can't see any way out. Save us, or we are lost. Amen.

831 We're not just asking you, Lord, we're *begging* you: hear our prayer, and help us . . . please! Amen.

Voice of God

see also Call of God; Prayer

832 Father God, forgive us, for, time after time, we put you on hold, making room for you when it suits us but then turning to other things, forgetting you are even there. Whatever we're doing, wherever we are, help us to stay connected – ready to listen to your voice and respond. Amen.

833 Almighty God, help us to hear, not with our ears but with our hearts – to hear your voice in those around us, your word in prayer and worship, your call in the daily routine, your speech in the miracle of life. Remind us of the many ways you speak, and give us a receptive spirit to hear what you are saying. Amen.

834 Sovereign God, we find it hard to hear you. Though you repeatedly speak – calling, teaching, confronting and encouraging – we get but a fraction of the message, the occasional snippet in what is otherwise a sea of noise. Open our hearts to you, so that we may be more on your wavelength – receptive to your word and responsive to your voice. Amen.

835 Speak your word, Lord, for we're listening – eager, attentive, hungry to hear your voice and to respond. Amen.

836 Loving God, we have ears for some things but not others, listening to what pleases us and shutting out the rest. In the noise and bustle of this world, help us to hear your voice. Amen.

837 We're ready, Lord, waiting for your instructions, eager to respond. Your word is our command. Tell us what we should do. Amen.

838 Loving God, teach us that we must listen if we would catch your voice, and look if we would glimpse your presence. Open our eyes to see, our ears to hear, our minds to understand and our hearts to respond. Amen.

839 Father God, forgive us, for we closed our ears to you, shutting out what we'd rather not hear. However unwelcome your message may be, help us to face it. Amen.

840 Apologies, Lord, for you speak but we fail to recognise your call. Help us to listen and to hear your voice. Amen.

841 Gracious God, though you speak in a multitude of ways, we're poor at getting the message, either failing to listen or getting our wires crossed. We confuse what we want you to say with what you've actually said, our lives, in consequence, becoming a shadow of what they should be, marred by shallow mistakes and deeper faults. Forgive us, and give us ears to hear and a heart to respond. Amen.

842 Eternal God, thank you that, as you have spoken in the past, so you continue to speak today; that though your word is old it is ever new. Amen.

843 Loving God, we try to listen, to hear what you have to say, but the message doesn't get through, at least not as clearly as we'd like. Speak again, and help us to hear. Amen.

Wisdom, seeking

844 All-seeing God, forgive us, for too often we fail to consider the consequences of our actions, jumping in with both feet and finding ourselves as a result in desperate situations from which there seems no escape. Teach us, before jumping into anything too deeply, to consider first how we'll get out of it, and when we make wrong decisions, come to our aid and save us from our folly. Amen.

845 Creator God, teach us to use rather than abuse your gifts, to enjoy them in moderation rather than excess. And help us to understand that some must be handled with care, or else they will consume us instead of us them. Amen.

846 Help us, Lord, for we make mountains out of molehills, magnifying little things out of all proportion until we can see nothing else. Teach us to focus on you, and to get a proper perspective on all. Amen.

847 Father God, forgive us, for we're too inquisitive for our own good, poking our noses into what doesn't concern us. Remind us that there's a place for healthy curiosity, but also for minding our own business, and help us to get each in its proper place. Amen.

848 Almighty God, give us wisdom to know you, intelligence to understand you better, perception to grasp your will, and discernment to follow you more faithfully. Amen.

849 God of all, teach us that there is a time and place for everything: for action . . . and restraint, for taking risks . . . and showing caution, for enthusiasm . . . and patience, for abandonment . . . and self-discipline. Help us to know which is which, and to get the balance right. Amen.

850 Lord Jesus Christ, too often we try to run before we can walk, and our feet slip from under us. In life, and in faith, give us patience to take one step at a time. Amen.

851 Creator God, help us to respect your gifts and treat them wisely, conscious that they may be a blessing or a curse, a treasure or a toxin. Help us to celebrate all you have given, but to use rather than abuse it. Amen.

852 Loving Lord, we have our dreams, our aspirations for the future, but not all our goals can become reality. Help us to recognise what we *can* do and what we *can't*. Amen.

853 God of grace, like everyone we can do *some* things by ourselves, but not all, for as well as strengths we have weaknesses, as well as skills, deficiencies. Teach us to know which is which: to tackle what we *can* do but admit to what we *can't*. Amen.

854 Loving God, give us wisdom in administering our finances – honesty and integrity. Save us, in investing our money, from inadvertently selling our souls. Amen.

855 Merciful God, forgive us, for we look at some things more deeply than we should, brooding on the trivial and insignificant. Teach us to focus on what really matters, and to leave the rest to you. Amen.

856 Lord of all, teach us that we can't sit on the fence for ever, that your love demands a response – for or against. Help us to make up our minds. Amen.

857 Living God, whether we write, read, talk or listen, alert us to the power of words, and help us to use them wisely. Teach us to think before we speak and to consider what we hear, that words may be a friend rather than foe, bringing pleasure instead of pain, light instead of darkness. Amen.

858 Lord Jesus Christ, there are things we *can* do and things we *can't*; challenges we're equipped to face and others beyond us. Help us to know the difference. Amen.

859 Sovereign God, when we seek our own way instead of yours, pleasure on earth instead of treasure in heaven, teach us to stop before it's too late – to turn back, and follow you. Amen.

860 We like to think we're wise, Lord – that we know all there is to know – but in reality we understand so little. Open our minds to find in you the true meaning of life. Amen.

861 Gracious God, you do not *control* us, but have given instead the privilege, yet also responsibility, of answering for our own actions; of being able, at least in part, to shape our own destiny. Help us to do so wisely and thoughtfully, mindful of you and others. Give us humility to respond to your guidance but also courage to stand on our own two feet, aware of what we *can* do and seeking your help in what we *can't*. Amen.

862 Almighty God, remind us that in all kinds of ways we reap what we sow, for better or for worse, words and deeds long buried bursting into life, bringing joy or sorrow, satisfaction or shame. Before we speak or act then, teach us to pause and ponder, lest in sowing the wind we reap the whirlwind. Amen.

863 Teach us, Lord, in whatever we think, say or do, to weigh things up first, considering them in the light, not of our wishes, but of *yours*. Amen.

864 All-seeing God, some say moral issues are simple, the right course of action being written in tablets of stone, but far from seeming black or white they can appear to us as shades of grey, what's right in one case seeming wrong in another. Grant wisdom and guidance to all facing complex moral decisions, and encircle in your everlasting arms those whose future depends upon them. Amen.

865 There are molehills in our lives, Lord – problems, trials and disagreements that get under our skin – but most of them are minor rather than major, a nuisance, nothing more. Forgive us for turning them into mountains, magnifying them out of all proportion until we can see nothing else. Give us, in all things, a proper sense of perspective, lest the biggest problem we face is ourselves. Amen.

866 Creator God, you've given us brains, intelligence with which to shape our world and influence our destiny. Help us to use our minds for good and not for evil. Amen.

867 Too easily, Lord, we're deceived, taken in by appearances. Forgive us, and help us to understand that not everything is as it seems. Amen.

868 Almighty God, we wish all choices were easy, swift and straightforward to deal with, but they're not, most being far more complex – what seems right to some seeming wrong to others. Give us wisdom then, in all our decisions, and, above all, the courage we need both to make them and to amend them when we get them wrong. Amen.

869 Father God, when life is complicated, bringing too many balls to juggle with, teach us to take one thing at a time, and to leave the rest with you. Amen.

Witnessing to Christ

870 Lord Jesus Christ, are we proud to be linked with you, ready to show where our loyalties lie? Or are we closet disciples, hiding our faith away for fear of what others might think should they know where we truly stand? Teach us never to be ashamed of you, lest the day come when we find you ashamed of us. Amen.

871 Loving God, help us to point to the way of Christ, so that others in turn may find guidance in their journey of life. May all we say, do, think and are point away from us and towards him. Amen.

872 Father God, what do we sound like when we speak of you? Are the terms we use easy to understand, anchored in daily life? Do we even know what we're trying to say? So often we use words unthinkingly, repeating parrot-fashion what we've heard from others, spouting pretentious clichés, pious guff. Teach us, rather than simply talking, to talk simply. Amen.

873 Lord Jesus Christ, make our lives a sign to others, an emblem of your love, pointing to your kingdom and speaking unmistakably of you. Amen.

874 God of grace, teach us to hold aloft the torch of faith, bearing it with pride and fervour. Help us to do our bit, through word and deed faithfully handing it on, so that others might receive and pass it on in turn: a flame of love, symbol of hope and beacon of truth – light for all the world. Amen.

875 Lord of all, teach us to witness authentically to you, speaking from personal experience of what we've found to be true. Help us to bring to life the reality of your love, telling of the blessings you've given, guidance offered, mercy shown and peace imparted. You have given us good news, glad tidings for all. Help us to share it. Amen.

876 Living Lord, though we wear no badge and bear no label, may something in our lives speak of you, testifying to the love you show, the forgiveness you offer and the peace you impart. Help us to point unmistakably to your life-changing grace. Amen.

877 Gracious God, what mark will we leave when our course is run? What imprint will we have made on human hearts? Help us to live in such a way that our words and deeds speak of you, testament not to our brief span but to your eternal love, and may that be legacy enough. Amen.

878 God of love, you call us to hand on to others the message we've received, but too often we betray that trust, keeping to ourselves what we should have shared, going it alone and forgetting the bigger picture. Forgive us and help us to play our part in your purpose, running our race faithfully, so that others may run theirs in turn. Amen.

879 Father God, pardon us, for we've been ashamed of you, whispering the good news of Christ as though it's a guilty secret, when we should have shouted it from the rooftops. Save us from timid witness and ineffectual commitment. Amen.

880 Living God, you have given us good news, the message of your love in Christ. Wherever the opportunity arises, teach us to share it. Amen.

881 Lord Jesus Christ, you call us to fish for people, winning hearts for you, but too often we leave it to others, not knowing where to start. Forgive us, and, however ill-equipped we feel, help us to take the plunge. Amen.

Worth of all

see also Judging others; Relationships

882 God of all, thank you that, in your eyes, no one is first or second class; that there is no elite few elevated at the expense of others. Thank you that, whatever their station in life, you treat everyone equally, reaching out in love and inviting a response. Teach us not to think too much of ourselves, but also not to think too little, remembering instead that you value us, and all. Amen.

883 Loving Lord, remind us that whoever we are, great or small, weak or strong, you value us equally, each having a place in your purpose. Amen.

884 Creator God, forgive us for overlooking the worth of others, seeing them as part of a nameless crowd rather than individuals, objects instead of people. Forgive us for dismissing what we don't understand, closing our eyes and ears to what is outside our experience or challenges our preconceptions. Open our hearts to the true value of all. Amen.

885 Lord of all, have mercy upon us, for we look down sometimes on others, valuing *them* too little and *ourselves* too much. Too often, and without good reason, we put on airs and graces, holding a misplaced sense of our own importance. Give us an understanding of the true worth of all, *us* included, having neither too low nor too high an opinion of any. Amen.

886 Father God, in a world where so many feel left on the scrapheap, discarded by society and of no use to anyone, teach us to see the worth not just of objects but equally of people. Open our eyes to look more deeply, recognising the gifts, qualities and potential of those around us, and, wherever we can, help us to nurture them, so that they may bloom again. Remind us that *you* value everyone, and help us to do the same. Amen.

887 Lord Jesus Christ, thank you that, whoever we are, and whatever our place in the world, each of us matters to you: that we are all unique and special individuals, precious in your sight. Teach us to respect ourselves and others, seeing, as you do, beneath the labels to the person underneath. Amen.

888 Loving God, not everything or everyone is to our liking, but save us from dismissing the worth of that which doesn't fit our criteria. Help us to respect the value of others and their right to see things differently than we do; to understand that beauty is in the eye of the beholder and that, just because we fail to see it, doesn't mean it isn't there. Amen.

889 Lord of all, reach out to those behind the statistics: the mother whose partner has walked out on her and the children, the worker whose factory has closed down, the trader whose business has folded, the victim of the industrial accident, the manager made redundant, the casual labourer whose services are no longer required. However hopeless they may feel, however disheartened, disillusioned or despondent, assure them of their worth as individuals, and help us as a society to do the same. Amen.

890 God of grace, forgive us, for we judge people by what we see, too often failing to delve deeper, and, in consequence, we miss hidden gems, the pearl within the oyster. Teach us never to dismiss anyone, however ordinary they may seem. Open our hearts instead to the value in all. Amen.

891 Lord Jesus Christ, remind us that people are different, no two precisely the same; that though we have some things in common, none of us can simply be lumped together, labelled as being of a certain type or particular kind. Teach us to recognise the individuality of all, and to respect each person we meet for who they are. Amen.

892 Creator God, save us, as individuals or as a society, from treating people as objects to be exploited, statistics processed, consumers targeted, resources managed. Remind us that in your eyes we are unique and precious, valued for who we are, each seen not as an object but as a person. Help us, then, in our dealings with others, to see behind the labels and to recognise the intrinsic worth of all. Amen.

893 Lord Jesus Christ, thank you for seeing beneath the surface to who we really are; for focusing not on the ugliness that disfigures our lives but recognising instead someone of infinite worth, precious enough for you to die for. Teach us, in turn, to see the good in others – the best rather than the worst – looking beyond appearances to the beauty hidden in all. Amen.

894 Merciful God, forgive us, for we look down on others, valuing *them* too little and *ourselves* too much. Teach us to be open to the true worth of all, having neither too low nor too high an opinion of any. Amen.

895 Gracious God, teach us to stand tall, in full assurance of our worth. However ordinary we may be or average feel, help us to respect ourselves, recognising that you value us as you value *all*. Amen.

Other **Nick Fawcett** books

Daily Prayer

1500975

www.kevinmayhew.com

2000 Prayers for Public Worship

1501101

www.kevinmayhew.com